Disarm and Disable

The Active Shooter Defense Guide

Joseph B. Walker

This book is a work of non-fiction. Unless otherwise noted, the author and the publisher make no explicit guarantees as to the accuracy of the information contained in this book and in some cases, names of people and places have been altered to protect their privacy.

Archway Publishing books may be ordered through booksellers or by contacting:

Archway Publishing
1663 Liberty Drive
Bloomington, IN 47403
www.archwaypublishing.com
1 (888) 242-5904

Because of the dynamic nature of the Internet, any web addresses or links contained in this book may have changed since publication and may no longer be valid. The views expressed in this work are solely those of the author and do not necessarily reflect the views of the publisher, and the publisher hereby disclaims any responsibility for them.

Interior Image Credit: Derek Kroshus and Terri Svetich

ISBN: 978-1-4808-8946-0 (sc)
ISBN: 978-1-4808-8947-7 (e)

Library of Congress Control Number: 2020905382

Print information available on the last page.

Archway Publishing rev. date: 3/25/2020

Table of Contents

....

Dedication

I dedicate this book to the countless victims and survivors of every active shooter. May God bless all of those who have experienced these horrible tragedies. I pray not only for them but also for their loved ones who have had to cope with their losses as they were forced to experience extreme and senseless acts of violence. The blame is solely on the shooters for these uncaring monsters would rather inflict pain on innocent people than deal with their own personal inadequacies. I would like to commend those dedicated first responders who continue to place themselves in harm's way to respond to these deadly locations to save lives. I further dedicate this work to everyone who can use any part of the information contained from cover to cover to keep them safe, regardless of whether they ever find themselves in a deadly environment, or are taking proactive steps on a daily basis to increase their safety from an active shooter.

Part One
Purpose

....

I instructed an Active Shooter Defense class in Las Vegas, Nevada teaching the students to **disarm and disable** the active shooter. Several months after the class, the promoter for the class sent me this email from a student who attended the class.

> "I wanted to thank you and Joey for the training last year. Last weekend I was at a Father's Day BBQ and someone who had a little too much to drink got into a fight. Shortly after I broke up the fight the guy went to his truck and pulled out a firearm. Being the closest one to him and utilizing what Joey had trained, I was able to disarm him immediately after he chambered a round. Out of all the people in the class I wouldn't have dreamed it would be me who found themselves in this situation, but Joey's training came right out of me without my brain registering what I was doing. So, thank you and thanks to him."

This is exactly why I do what I do in training people to take part in saving their own life and potentially the lives of others around them. As you read this guide, know that every part of my being believes that with knowledge and confidence, people can make a difference (whether armed or unarmed) in saving lives and the overall outcome of an armed person or an active shooter.

Active shootings can take a few seconds or last a protracted period of time. Most active shooters seldom use entirely new tactics, but rely on using the tactics from prior cases. The techniques and tactics in this guide utilize my training in the Martial Arts and law enforcement experiences over my career and beyond. It is imperative for those who wish to survive and active shooting to look at potentially dangerous situations and see the reality of the threat, consider the plausible resolutions and then quickly implement the best strategies or tactics to overcome the threat. This publication is meant as a companion to my book "Shots Fired: Surviving an Active Shooter/Assailant." "Disarm and Disable" is not only a philosophy, but a strategy in dealing with any active shooter. The defender (whether armed or unarmed) should immediately recognize the deadly threat whenever shots are fired or an active shooter appears, and take the required steps to either escape from the immediate area, or if escape is not possible and when/if the opportunity arises to ambush the shooter, disarm and disable him/her expeditiously saving their own life and possibly the lives of others.

This guide has three main purposes: to **provide some of the essential material** addressed in my previous book; to **highlight some of the most significant Active shooting cases** that have transpired since the initial book was published; and to **offer enhanced tactics and techniques to <u>counterattack active shooters</u>**. I have also provided applicable photographs to bring clarity to the various positional firearm disarming and ambush strategies and techniques.

The most significant Active shootings cases are: A sniper style shooting at the **Mandalay Bay Concert** in Las Vegas, Nevada that occurred on October 1, 2017. The **Marjory Stoneman Douglas High** school shooting in Parkland, Florida that occurred on February 14, 2018. A restaurant shooting at **The Waffle House** in Antioch, Tennessee that occurred on April 22, 2018. The **Henry Platt**

Company workplace shooting in Aurora, Illinois that occurred on February 15, 2019. Shootings that occurred at two different Mosque locations carried out by the same shooter in **the city of Christchurch, New Zealand** that occurred on March 15, 2019. The Tram **Utrecht, Netherlands** shooting that occurred on March 18, 2019. The **Virginia Beach,** Virginia workplace shooting that occurred on May 31, 2019. The **Gilroy Garlic Festival** shooting in Gilroy, California that occurred on July 28, 2019. The **El Paso,** Texas **Wal-Mart** shooting that occurred on August 3, 2019. The **Dayton, Ohio Oregon district** shooting that occurred on August 4, 2019. The **West Freeway Church of Christ** shooting in White Settlement, Texas that occurred on December 29, 2019. The **Greyhound bus** shooting while the bus was in transit from Los Angeles, California that occurred on February 3, 2020 and the **Suatham Phithak Military Camp** and **Terminal 21 Mall** shootings in Nakhon Ratchasima, Thailand that occurred on February 8, 2020.

1.   Mandalay Bay Concert, Las Vegas, Nevada, October 1, 2017

A gunman opened fire using various weapons, some equipped with a "bump stock," from the thirty-second floor of the Mandalay Bay Resort and Casino. A bump stock allows a semiautomatic firearm to operate in an almost fully automatic rate of fire. The footage of the shooting and the sound of the weapon firing appeared to be firing not on semiautomatic but in fully automatic rate of fire.

It appeared at first that concertgoers were mostly unaware of the danger that was raining down on them from above. When victims of gunfire began to fall around them, it quickly became aware that someone was shooting them. From talking with friends who were attending the concert, at first it could not be determined where the gunshots were coming from. Once it was discovered that the shots were being fired from the Mandalay Bay hotel suite overlooking the concert venue, potential victims were able to make choices as to how to escape or shelter from the sniper fire.

Las Vegas Metropolitan Police and the casino security cautiously and expeditiously made their way to the shooter's hotel suite. Upon entering the shooter's suite, the shooter's final act was to take his own life. In the end, the shooter sprayed nearly 1,100 rounds down onto concertgoers outside his hotel suite, killing fifty-nine people and wounding over eight hundred people. This shooting was the largest mass killing sniper-style attack since the 1966 University of Texas shooting (Austin, Texas), where sixteen innocent people were killed.

Tactics:

- The tactics to escape any type of sniper style shooting is to first notice when the gunshots are fired, notice where they are being fired from, and determine the direction where the hail of bullets are going. If you have determined that you are possibly within the kill zone, get down as close to the ground as possible to present a smaller target. You have two main options: escape from the kill zone or seek cover from the bullets that may be fired at you. If you have located the approximate location of the shooter and the directions the shots are being fired toward, that may highlight a path and allow you to escape.

- You should have previously located your exits and places for temporary cover (not just from a sniper-style attack but also from a shooter appearing at ground level) as you enter every environment.

- If escape is not immediately available, you will need to seek cover from behind or under something that will prevent the rounds being fired at you from hitting you. When shots are not being fired in your direction, take the opportunity to either move to a better place of cover or effect a total escape from the area. Once you have escaped the initial kill zone, place at least one or more structures between you and the last known location of the shooter.

- Once you have escaped to a place of safety, check yourself and others who may be with you to determine if first aid lifesaving measures need to be used.
- Venues that host special events, concerts, sporting events, and so forth, should coordinate with active duty and retired law enforcement personnel who will attend their venues. These armed and highly trained personnel could meet in the venue's security office one hour prior to the doors opening.
- This meeting has the purpose of allowing venue staff to meet all the law enforcement (active duty and retired personnel) who are armed individuals to have a face-to-face meeting and see one another, obtain clothing descriptions and their relative seating positions within the venue. In the unlikely event that an active shooter begins his or her shooting, these armed force multipliers could utilize the "Don't Shoot Me" (DSM) banners that were discussed in my previous book. Once those banners are deployed, these members could immediately engage the shooter with little fear of being seen as another bad guy and have a direct effect on the number of casualties the shooter might be able to amass.

2. Marjory Stoneman Douglas High School, Parkland, Florida, February 14, 2018

A former student who had been expelled from the school for his threatening behavior returned to the school. Once inside, the killer moved throughout all three floors of the building, shooting and killing students and faculty along the way. At one point, the shooter activated the fire alarm to shoot those who had emptied out into the school's hallways. In all, seventeen students and staff members were shot and killed by the shooter, who used an AR-15 style rifle for his attack. After the shooting, the suspect discarded his weapon, raised his hands over his head, and blended in with the other students as they evacuated from the school.

Tactics:

- When some of the first shots were fired, several of the faculty as well as students believed it was an active shooter drill being conducted by the school. It appears that the school had (or at least expected) this type of active shooter training. This confusion on the staff and students brought about hesitation that may have caused lives to be lost. <u>No entity should employ active shooter defense training that is a surprise</u>. All training should be well-coordinated and prearranged having been announced to staff several days prior and the day of the training. If gunshots are fired (for familiarization purposes only), every person should know it is only a drill and a not a real threat to the lives and safety of the everyone present. <u>There should never be students present during any training if familiarization gunshots are to be used</u>. There should also be numerous safety officers dressed in safety vests and present throughout the venue to ensure the safety of all within that training environment.
- Each school should have an audible alarm (similar to those used in Oklahoma City, OK to warn of tornados). This audible alarm (and not the school's public address system) would be used warn everyone of an active shooter, allowing them to take the most appropriate safety precautions to save their own lives.
- The shooter never physically entered any classrooms but shot into the classrooms from the hallway through the glass window in the classroom doors. Students were able to take cover in a safe corner of the classroom, outside of the shooter's view.

- These safe corners should be clearly marked on the floor by a painted line.
- Install steel plates to reinforce the inside of each classroom's adjoining walls and the corners or side walls to prevent the shooter from firing shots through the walls of the classroom from the hallway or an adjacent room.
- Many schools have "lockdown" protocols where as soon as they are notified or aware of the deadly threat (or during drills) immediately begin to close and lock doors and bring students into classrooms if they notice students around their classroom door. If a student is not even assigned to that particular classroom and the student is near the classroom door, the student is brought into the classroom and the door is locked.
- There may be some students who are unable to enter a classroom to shelter in place and are in effect "caught out in the open" during a real active shooting event. When this occurs, students should be taught (by school officials or parents) to tactically exit the school at the safest exit points. Students should then go out into the community surrounding the school where they can summon help using their cellular phones.
- Upon hearing gunshots, some faculty members were either rushing to the area to determine what was occurring or standing in the hallway near the open door of a classroom. Training should provide instruction to faculty staff on how to tactically enter and exit a location when shots are fired. This includes how to peek around corners, enter and exit rooms, and the sounds a weapon makes when the shooter is either clearing a jammed weapon due to a malfunction, reloading the weapon, or transitioning to another weapon. This training could prevent someone from inadvertently entering a kill zone.
- Students in one class heard gunshots, but thought the sound was coming from an equipment cart used at the school. Any

piece of equipment that might be confused with the sound of gunshots should immediately be replaced.

- The shooter activated the fire alarm, causing students to leave their classrooms for a perceived fire drill to have a target-rich environment where he could engage students in the hallways instead of entering classrooms. All fire drills should be announced in advance, where all faculty members are aware of the date and exact time of the drill. Any audible alert outside of an advanced notification should be viewed as suspect. If at any time during an actual prearranged fire drill should a real-world threat occur, all faculty and staff should be able to alert others of the real threat and take the necessary steps to safeguard lives. In the event the fire alarm is ever activated, each teacher should take the time to determine the validity of the fire alarm.

- If the threat of a fire is real, each person should react accordingly. If the threat cannot be validated, teachers and students should remain in their respective classrooms or other safe areas with their doors locked from the outside. All second and third story classrooms should have at least two evacuation ladders that can be deployed in the event the traditional exit of the classroom is not possible.

- The county sheriff's deputy whose regular duty assignment was the school law enforcement resource officer, failed to take the necessary actions to enter the building and engage the shooter. Law enforcement will ultimately respond in huge numbers to the scene of an active shooter. In many cases, the typical response time for armed law enforcement personnel will be at least several minutes before their arrival. Regardless of what others are "supposed" to do during an active shooting, each faculty and staff member (from the school principal to the custodian) should know how to take the necessary steps to keep themselves and others safe from an active shooter.

- Do whatever you can to take part in saving your own life, whether that is to take direct physical action against the shooter/assailant if he or she is in your immediate area or to lay in wait and ambush the shooter/assailant should the shooter breach your concealed location.

3. Waffle House Shooting, Antioch, Tennessee, April 22, 2018

The gunman used an AR-15 style rifle as he approached the Waffle House, where he shot and killed four people. A patron inside the restaurant ambushed the shooter and disarmed him of his weapon. The killer fled the restaurant and was apprehended the following day.
Tactics:

- What is most notable in this event is that a patron inside the restaurant, a twenty-nine-year-old man with no formal self-defense training, was able to ambush the shooter and disarm him. We now know that a person with little or no active shooter defense training can and did successfully ambush a shooter, disarm him and have a direct effect on saving his own life and potentially the lives of others. This is a great advertisement for all concerned about learning to defend themselves using physical techniques and tactics to disarm and disable an active shooter/assailant when required to save their own life.

4. Henry Pratt Co. Shooting, Aurora, Illinois, February 15, 2019

An employee with fifteen years on the job was called into a meeting with his company's human resource manager and two other employees. The purpose of the meeting was to complete the termination of this fifteen-year employee. Instead, the employee produced a semiautomatic handgun and shot and killed the people in that meeting. The employee exited the meeting room and shot and killed two other employees.

Other employees reported that the shooter was armed with a handgun equipped with a laser sight. When police responded, they exchanged fire with the gunman, resulting in six police officers being injured. Of those injured officers, four sustained gunshot wounds, the fifth officer sustained injuries from shrapnel, and the sixth officer sustained injuries while responding to the shooting scene. The deadly altercation between police and the armed gunman lasted approximately ninety minutes and resulted in the police killing the gunman.

The shooter (former employee) had a significant criminal history from at least two different states. When the shooter purchased a firearm in Illinois prior to the confrontation with his employment managers, nothing was flagged in his criminal history. It was not until the shooter applied for a concealed carry permit that his criminal past was discovered. The law enforcement agency mailed the shooter a letter to advise his concealed carry permit would not be approved and that he should surrender the firearm he had purchased.

Tactics:

- First, whenever an employee is brought into any meeting with management where discipline or discharge may be an issue, management and first-line supervisors of the employee should use caution. The employee may or may not display, or management fails to see or take steps on pre-event indictors signaling a propensity for violence.

Nevertheless, management should always consider that violence (armed or unarmed) could result whenever significant discipline (suspension or leave with or without pay) or discharge are considered. Never have a contentious meeting alone with a hostile or potentially hostile employee. As the employee enters the meeting, notice if the employee has brought or left positioned, anything into the meeting, such as a duffel bag, backpack, purse, lunch bag, or anything large enough to conceal a firearm.

- Second, give a cursory look of the employee's body in places where a firearm could be concealed. Places such as the pockets, waistband, ankles, calf, and underneath the armpits are all places where handguns may be holstered or concealed. Keep in mind that there are clothing items that are specifically designed to conceal a firearm inside pockets. If you notice the presence of a weapon, this is the time for diplomacy. Politely and immediately stop the meeting, excuse yourself and others from the meeting, and initiate your protocol for an armed person or employee with an unauthorized firearm on the premises. Those protocols may require an evacuation, shelter, or lockdown in place—or any other appropriate action to safeguard innocent lives. Do not confront the employee or let the armed employee know that you are aware of a firearm in their possession.
- Third, consider a protocol for the discipline and/or discharge of an employee who is hostile. Some of these measures may include armed security or a law enforcement presence during any face-to-face contact with the hostile employee.
- Consider all communications with the hostile employee via documents sent through email or through certified mail. Also, consider telephone conferencing with that employee. Check your local laws to ascertain the legality of recording the audio of the telephone call, ensuring you are advising all parties to the telephone call that the call is being recorded.

5.   Mosque Shootings, Christchurch, New Zealand, March 15, 2019

A self-described white supremacist was reported to have at least one AR-15 style rifle. The shooter entered a Muslim mosque wearing black clothing and a helmet and began shooting into the crowd without discriminating between killing men, women, or children.

The shooter killed approximately fifty people at two different mosques. What is significant about this shooting is that the killer livestreamed the shooting over social media so that many people would be able to view the carnage.

Active shooters will often try something to bring even more notoriety to their crimes. They may try to increase the number of people killed, the method of killing, or add a new twist that has not been done before. In this case, the shooter went to two different locations and livestreamed the shootings over social media.

Tactics:

- Having an armed and trained ministry security team on duty every time any house of worship is in session should be the first step. It has been repeatedly demonstrated that active shooters have and continue to approach, enter, and shoot unsuspecting members, sometimes under the guise of seeking worship.
- Any such team should be comprised of members that can adequately address any active shooter/assailant and is a huge advantage in protecting all those at a place of worship. The congregation needs to also be advised to follow the directions of their security team. Congregants should be briefed on the *run, hide, ambush* strategies.
- The "run" portion does not mean they have to run to escape through the front door. They can also escape through other locations of egress, such as through side or rear doors. Also

consider unconventional exits such as windows a means of escape.

- The "hide" portion of the strategy was so literally taken that in other church shootings, members of the congregation hid underneath their seats; which is where their bodies were found. When choosing to hide, that location is meant to be temporary shelter until a better option is available, such as an escape route or finding a better place to hide. Remember, if you choose to hide, always be prepared to fight should the shooter/assailant breech and approaches your location.

- The "ambush" portion will have a physical component teaching their participants how to disarm or disable a shooter armed with a handgun, long gun, or edged weapon (knife, machete, or what have you).

- There are martial arts teachers and schools that can specialize in teaching students how to disarm a shooter armed with either a handgun, long gun, or edged weapon. There are also schools that have no plausible idea of how to disarms any weapon. When you visit a martial arts school, have a private conversation with the instructor. Ask the instructor to demonstrate (preferably on one of his or her students) some of the weapons disarming techniques for handguns, long guns, and edged weapons. If any of the technique are too convoluted, take more than a couple of movements to gain complete control of the weapon or their techniques and use tactics that are ridiculous, politely excuse yourself and seek another place for instruction.

6.   Tram Shooting, Utrecht, Netherlands, March 18, 2019

The occupants were inside a tram when a shooter opened fire. This tram shooting is reminiscent of the 1993 Long Island subway shooting.

The killer literally had his victims trapped so they could not run, had no place to hide, and were trapped with their shooter unarmed.

Tactics:

- Countries, cities, and other entities need to understand that when they disarm the populace and/or place signage that specifically forbids the possession of a firearm, killers will never be deterred by such laws, which places the populace totally at the mercy of their attacker. The governing body must allow the lawful ability to possess a firearm to fight fire with fire, literally. Every governing body should allow (not forbid) and license its citizens to legally arm themselves for the sole purpose of protecting themselves against an armed assailant.
- Whenever any entity requires persons to enter or be within an area and they are not allowed to legally carry their concealed firearms, that entity should be prepared to provide adequate armed security that can protect against an armed assailant. Ultimately, it is the responsibility of all individuals to seek instruction in self-defense methods that will allow them to effectively and efficiently disarm and disable an attacker.

7. Municipal Complex Shooting, Virginia Beach, Virginia, May 31, 2019

A reportedly quiet forty-year-old man employed as a civil engineer with Virginia Beach, with fifteen years on the job and no known work discipline issues, emailed his resignation from his job earlier that day. Near the end of that day, the man walked into his former worksite and began firing upon his former supervisors and coworkers. The shooter was armed with two .45-caliber handguns and numerous rounds of ammunition. The shooter killed twelve people, eleven of whom were his coworkers and a contractor. Once police arrived, they engaged the suspect in a sustained gun battle, resulting in one officer being wounded and the suspect shot and killed by police.

Tactics:

- One of the city employees who was inside the building during the shooting heard the gunshots as they were being fired by the shooter and thought the shots were not a real event occurring but just another active shooter drill. <u>Civilian active shooter training should not involve the surprise firing of rounds, nor should there ever be any confusion among employees as to if the sounds of gunshots are an active shooter training or a real event.</u> If unexpected gunshots are heard (notwithstanding announced training of gunshot familiarization training) every person hearing those shots should know without any doubt that the shooting is the real thing and to take immediate lifesaving actions.

- All options for your survival are contingent upon the location of the shooter/assailant and your exact location. Whether you opt to escape or shelter in place, help those who are within your area. It is not recommended to go back into a kill zone to save additional people. Doing so is equivalent to running back into a burning building to save others. You may or may not be successful.

8.   Gilroy Garlic Festival, Gilroy, California, July 28, 2019

A gunman was able to circumvent all security measures for the garlic festival and enter the area by cutting a hole in the chain-link fence that surrounded the special event. The gunman then entered the festival grounds and used a semiautomatic rifle to shoot indiscriminately into the crowd, killing three people (one a six-year-old boy) and wounding at least fifteen others. Once police engaged the shooter, the shooter took his own life. What stands out about this shooting is that the shooter did not access the event grounds via any normal entry gate but gained entry through the chain-link fence, out of the normal view of security.

Tactics:

- The gunman selected to cut through and enter an area of the perimeter fence out of the view of the event's security to gain entry into the event grounds, bypassing controlled access points. All areas of the perimeter need to be capable of being secured not only by a physical barrier but also by personal observation and/or electronic technology.
- Security personnel conduct screening of a special event that usually consists of checking inside women's purses and backpacks. Weapons screening should consist either of walk-through metal detectors and hand wands, not just a visual observation of a person.
- The shooter began shooting in broad daylight. Everyone attending any type of event should always have identified several areas where they can escape to inside the event for temporary cover or have identified which exits are best to cover their escape.
- The shooter attacked people out in the open. A lone shooter is incapable of watching every angle of his or her own body when they are engaged in an attack. Look for the opportunity to exploit the shooter's blindside by using an improvised weapon.
- Well in advance of an attack, locate potential improvised weapons to use against the shooter/assailant (such as a kitchen knife or even a metal fork). These items may be obtained from food vendors at the event.
- The event had live music, and one artist had begun their music set. Once the shooting started, some festival attendees thought the gunfire might have been fireworks. Each event and venue should have an audible alarm (similar to those used in Oklahoma City, OK to warn of tornados) that can be heard

over any music or public-address system. This audible alarm would warn event attendees and staff working the event of an active shooter, allowing them to take the most appropriate safety precautions to save their own lives.

- Family members are sometimes separated by choice, as one or more may use the restroom, go to another area for a different food venue, or for many other reasons. If you are there with your family, do what you can to all stay together. If you elect to not all stay together, identify and communicate a primary and secondary family reunification area.

- Law enforcement or another professional with expertise in active shooter defense should conduct a vulnerability assessment to address all physical security measures.

- Attract, allow and schedule armed retired and active off-duty plainclothes law enforcement to cover each day and hour to ensure adequate coverage. This will allow numerous legally armed and trained plainclothes personnel to be inside and outside the event. If circumstances force those legally armed personnel at the event to become activated, each person, upon notification of the shooting, could deploy their DSM banners to avoid friendly fire. On-duty and uniformed personnel responding to such an event would immediately identify these authorized armed individuals.

- Special events usually have a meeting with the agencies within that jurisdiction, at which time the law enforcement agency could advise of the plan to use retired, active duty, off-duty plainclothes law enforcement personnel to support their event.

9. Walmart Shooting, El Paso, Texas, August 3, 2019

On a busy Saturday morning, a lone gunman appeared in the parking lot and, using a semiautomatic rifle, shot and killed twenty-two people in the span of just a few minutes. The police responded and were able to take the young adult male into custody without further incident.

Tactics:

- The gunman was reported to have initially fired upon people in the parking lot and blocked their vehicular exit. Always have several avenues of escape, even if you must drive over landscape or other custom curbing.
- If escaping by vehicle is not an option, be capable of escaping on foot. Go in the opposite direction of the shooter and do what you can to keep objects between you and the shooter.
- If you think you may be targeted by the shooter, move in a perpendicular erratic zigzag fashion as you escape from the shooter. Moving in this fashion will make it more difficult for the shooter to track and predict your escape movements.
- When you are on foot in a parking lot, stay low and keep one or more vehicles between you and the last known location of the shooter. You may initially need to move as fast as you can on your hands and feet instead of a standing position in an all-out sprint.
- If you are not capable of having a visual of the shooter, listen to the sounds of gunfire, which will provide the shooter's location.
- If you use temporary cover behind a vehicle or any other object and are unable to have a view on the shooter, you may be able to perform a quick peek to ascertain the location of the shooter. A quick peek should last only one to two seconds but may give you a glimpse of the shooter's actions.
- Once the gunfire stops, try to determine if the shooter is experiencing a malfunction of his weapon, reloading his weapon, or transitioning to another weapon. Any of these may be the best time to escape or if close enough, ambush the shooter.

- If you are being fired upon, find something to hide behind (also known as cover). You may even hear the rounds fired from the suspect's weapon striking surfaces around you.
- You might be able to determine if the shooter is moving closer to your location by listening to the sound (also known as the report) from the shooter's weapon getting louder.
- Workers inside the store as well as inside one fast-food restaurant hid behind counters and other areas and waited for the shots to stop being fired. Remember, just hiding keeps you in the kill zone longer, but escaping from the entire area allows you to get outside of the kill zone. Don't worry about your employment by staying behind to safeguard money or property, take steps to survive the shooting!
- When you are in public, play the "what if" game. Imagine a shooter in a specific location and what your reactions would be if shots were being fired. Look at your avenues of escape or the best places to ambush the shooter.
- If you are legally armed, ensure the handgun you are carrying has sufficient knockdown power that is designed to stop the shooter's aggression.
- Make sure you also have sufficient ammunition in case you need to reload.
- Ensure that you are capable of taking precise shots on the shooter to stop the shooter.
- Be aware that you can legally use lethal option on the shooter, as you are now acting in the defense of others.
- Know that you can "shoot to stop" the killer and have permission to fire upon the shooter regardless of the angle of counterattack is from the shooter's side or behind him/her. You are never legally compelled to be face to face or warn a killer who is using deadly force.

- Beware of responding law enforcement or other legally armed citizens who might be drawn to you if you have a firearm in your hands.
- If you are armed and have another person with you as you take lethal action against the shooter, have that person call 9-1-1 to advise the operator to broadcast that you are armed and about to engage the shooter. Have that person give the operator your physical description including your clothing and the shooter's description if known.
- If you are alone, you may need to multitask by calling 9-1-1 to advise of your actions, your physical description, as well as the shooter's description and exact location.
- If you are not legally armed and only if you are close enough to the shooter and are very experienced in weapons disarming techniques, use that break in the shooting to counterattack the shooter. Attack when the shooter is not looking directly at you!
- If you are not familiar with the sounds of gunshots being fired inside and outside of a building, visit your local firearms ranges to notice the different sounds of different caliber weapons.

10. Oregon District Shooting, Dayton, Ohio, August 4, 2019

A lone shooter armed with a semiautomatic rifle and wearing body armor descended upon the Oregon Historic District (a popular nightlife scene) area of Dayton, Ohio. The gunman opened fire upon patrons and was able to kill nine people, one of them his own sister. Surveillance footage of the area illustrated movements of potential victims as they ran for their lives. This same footage showed several vehicles driving down the street, appearing rather clueless as the gunman targeted pedestrians in that area. Dayton police expeditiously responded to the scene and engaged the shooter within thirty seconds of the first round being fired. The shooter did not survive this encounter.

This shooting was the third mass murder in the United States in a short period, prompting significant attention from many politicians. The usual discussions of gun control, mental health, and other possible contributing factors as well as the shooter's motive for engaging in his deadly rampage were debated among news stations, politicians, and anyone who thought they had something to contribute and wanted to weigh in on the issues. The bottom line is the bad guy obtained a firearm and committed murders of unsuspecting people in a public place.

Tactics:

- If you are driving in a vehicle and see people apparently in a panic and escaping from an area, determine what and why they are in such a hurry to escape.
- Refrain from allowing the volume of your vehicle's stereo to prevent you from hearing emergencies in progress outside your vehicle. Slightly rolling down one or more windows may allow you to hear what is transpiring just outside of your vehicle.
- Remember, if you are on foot and attempting to escape from a shooter, it may be best to run perpendicular and zigzag away with no discernable patter from the shooter as opposed to running in a straight line from the shooter. Moving in this fashion may make it more difficult for the shooter to track your movements or predict your escape movements.
- Stay low and keep one or more vehicles between you and the last known location of the shooter.
- You may initially need to move as fast as you can on your hands and feet instead of in a standing position in an all-out sprint.

11. West Freeway Church of Christ White Settlement, Texas, December 29, 2019

A man dressed in dark clothing was sitting in a pew during a church service. The man stood and approached the person who had just served him holy communion. The man in dark clothing produced a shotgun from underneath his clothing and shot one man. An armed congregant attempting to draw his handgun from his waistband was the next person shot. As other congregants reacted to the shots fired, another armed congregant (who was part of the church security team) drew his handgun and fired one round into the suspect. The suspect was neutralized. This is one of the best examples of how a well-trained and armed individual can use deadly force to stop an active shooter. Several of the congregants who were not part of the security team also drew their firearms but did not discharge any rounds.

TACTICS:

- Especially useful for Ministry Security teams, notice everyone who approaches and enters a house or worship (or any other environment) and make a quick assessment placing the person into one of three categories:
  - **Threat**
  - **No threat**
  - **Not sure**
- If the person is deemed a **threat**, take the immediate and necessary actions to stop the threat. The person is a threat if he/she is holding or being in possession of a deadly weapon (handgun, long gun, edged weapon) **and** that person appears to be an imminent threat to the lives and safety of others.
- Stopping the threat could be any appropriate use of force ranging from disarming the person, holding the armed suspect at gunpoint, to using the appropriate amount of force to stop the

person, i.e. firing on and into the suspect to stop their deadly act. Stopping the threat is best made by one or more persons who have the requisite training, justification, certification and legal authority on the property to use force.

- If the house of worship has an armed security team, members of that team (and not other congregants) should be the ones uniquely designated to use deadly force.
- Each armed member of the security team should attend training and display proficiency with their firearm on a consistent basis.
- Armed members of the security team should practice on the firing range drawing and firing while moving perpendicular to the target. Moving in this fashion may make it harder for the shooter to hit the armed security officer.
- It is imperative that armed security team members have specific areas of responsibilities and persons dedicated as the primary and secondary designated shooters that may fire on the threat. This will prevent unnecessary shots from being fired by security team members that might strike "friendly" targets.
- Designating a secondary shooter for the armed security team will provide an immediate backup should the primary designated shooter become incapacitated, or not at the best angle to take the shot on the threat.
- Whether your place of worship has an armed security team or not, if shots are fired while you are inside a church service, take the immediate steps to ensure your safety.
- The steps required to increase your safety will all be contingent on the location of the shooter relative to you. If you are not immediately in danger, get as low to the ground as possible. Standing up may place you in a direct path of the shooter, or return fire from anyone who is an armed church security team member as they take lethal action against the shooter.
- Standing up will also present a larger target for the shooter who may look at the next target of opportunity to shoot.

- If you are not in the immediate area of the shooter, escape if possible.
- <u>If escape is not possible</u> and <u>the shooter is close enough to touch with no one returning lethal fire to stop the shooter</u>, you should physically engage the shooter to <u>disarm and disable</u> him/her.
- If the person is deemed as **no threat**, no further action is required other than occasionally observing the person to verify the right assessment has been made.
- If the person is deemed as **not sure**, additional information is immediately required to either place the person into the **threat** or **no threat** category.
- Some of the information may be garnered by conversing with the person to determine the true motives as to why the person is attending service for that day.

12. Greyhound bus in transit between Los Angeles and Northern California, February 3, 2020

A Greyhound bus left Los Angeles, California, during the late-night early morning hours carrying an untold number of passengers. Approximately eighty miles north of their departure location, a male shooter shot and killed one person and wounded five others during his shooting spree. Several of the passengers on the bus were able to launch a counterattack on the shooter, disarming him of his handgun. The bus driver pulled the bus over to the side of the road where the shooter exited the bus. The bus driver drove on to the next feasible highway exit where he stopped to summon help for those who were shot by the gunman. This is a prime example where unarmed citizens take action to engage an armed man, disarm him and prevent the further loss of life.

TACTICS:

- Whenever you are inside a public conveyance (bus, train, tram, etc.) you are inside an environment where escape is not immediately possible.
- Locate the person who has begun their deadly rampage.
- If you choose to hide, this will not stop the shooter from continuing their deadly rampage.
- Because the ability to escape is not possible, the shooter needs to be expeditiously disarmed and disabled to prevent further injury or loss of life.
- If you are close to the shooter and he/she is not immediately firing in your direction, you must take immediate action to disarm and disable the shooter.

13. Suatham Phithak Military camp and Terminal 21 Mall Nakhon, Ratchasima, Thailand February 8, 2020

A Thai soldier shot and killed two people (his superior and a civilian) at the Suatham Phithak Military camp. After the shooting on the military camp, the shooter stole several weapons, ammunition and a vehicle and traveled to the Terminal 21 Mall in Nakhon Ratchasima, Thailand. While enroute to the mall, the shooter continued his rampage killing another twenty-seven people in a shooting spree in and around the mall. The police tweeted to shoppers still inside the seven-story mall "Please be calm, find a safe place to hide and mute your mobile phones." Police also advised them to send their locations, the number of people with them and their contact numbers to police. During the rampage, some shoppers who were still inside the mall and hiding from the shooter, as well as the shooter himself posted on social media. Sixteen hours after the ordeal began, the police announced the suspect had been fatally shot.

TACTICS:

- Whenever possible, explore all entrances and exits as possible avenues of escape for every building or shopping environment (inside and outside) in advance of any incident. In the unlikely event an immediate escape is required, you will have advanced knowledge of different routes to escape.
- Mentally play the "what if" game. Imagine that a person approximately 100 yards from where you are is holding a firearm in their hands. Imagine what actions you would take if that person were shooting at others whether inside or outside of the mall.
- As you walk to and through a shopping mall, notice places you could use for temporary cover and immediate avenues of escape if a gunman were to attack at that time and location.
- Go into several stores and without drawing attention to yourself, look to determine where the rear or side exits are located.
- Ascertain if the store's rear exit empties out into a hallway or to the exterior of the mall (outside). Do not open doors to the business as alarms may activate.
- If the rear or side exits empty into a hallway, notice if there is another door nearby that does exit to the exterior of the mall and out into an outside area.
- Inquire with your emergency dispatch facility if they have the ability to communicate critical information via cell phone.
- If they are not set up to communicate with you by text, you may need to text a relative or close friend who could relay critical information to law enforcement.

- Your ability to communicate by telephone may be limited, therefore be familiar with how to send out a group text to loved ones and close friends who could relay information to law enforcement.
- Never count on being able to get to your vehicle and exit the parking area as you may need to leave the entire area on foot. You may need to retrieve your vehicle and other property left behind once the scene is cleared by law enforcement.
- If you are on the outside of the mall, stay as low to the ground as possible and use parked vehicles as temporary cover.
- Weave between parked vehicles as you continue to move further out of the entire area.
- If you must stay hidden and restricted to an area, remember to silence your cell phone.
- Also, determine potential items that could be used as improvised weapons should you need to ambush the shooter.
- If you are legally in possession of a handgun, consider the best places you could use it if you need to deploy that weapon.
- Only draw your concealed handgun moments prior to the threat entering your immediate area. Prematurely drawing your handgun might lead others to believe that you are the actual shooter.

No two active shooter situations are exactly identical. All the tactics listed in the above shootings may be useful. It is best to **be familiar with all the tactics** mentioned and **employ the ones that best suit your particular set of circumstances**.

Part Two
Strategies

··

In the 1950s, school children were taught to hide under their desks from the possible fallout of a nuclear bomb blast. In the 1980s, school children were taught to hide under their desks from the threat of an earthquake or tornado. And in contemporary times, school children are being taught to hide under their own desks from an active shooter. Children as well as adults have been using school classroom desks, office furniture and hiding inside closets as the primary means of defense against an active shooter when other viable means of defense are available.

Most trainers who teach active shooter defense refer to _run, hide, fight_ but will intentionally gloss over the "fight" portion and provide little to no specific detail. If anything is mentioned, it is usually stated that victims should pick up a heavy object and throw it towards the person armed with a handgun, long gun, or edged weapon.

Since my initial publication, _Shots Fired_, was released, I have conducted numerous training courses and have met many people who were mandated to attend their company active shooter defense training classes taught by some other entity. Virtually all attendees from training classes provided by other vendors have yet to report that they were never taught how to properly ambush the shooters or properly disarm the shooters of their weapons.

Rather than parrot the phrase run, hide, fight, I now use the concept of *__run, hide, ambush__*! I teach students in my classes what law enforcement officers would do if they were in a similar situation whether armed or unarmed. Officers would not hide under furniture or inside a closet. We would decide on a physical course of action to ambush the shooter to **disarm and disable** him/her when the situation presents itself.

Quite a number of active shooters are armed with more than one weapon which could be a threat to your life and possibly the lives of others. Therefore, merely disarming the active shooter of the firearm they are using may not be sufficient to stop the shooter's rampage. Should the shooter charge or attempt to physically retrieve their firearm, or reach for a second deadly weapon, you may need to use deadly force and shoot the person with his/her own firearm. If you are legally carrying a concealed handgun, you may elect to use your handgun rather than the shooter's firearm. Besides, you know your handgun is operational 100 percent of the time. If there is more than one defender, the second defender may place the disarmed shooter into a carotid control hold where the shooter would be rendered unconscious, thereby disabling the shooter.

There are some school districts who have elected to arm schoolteachers with firearms. While some teachers may be able to quickly make the psychological paradigm shift from teacher to armed defender with the option of using deadly force, other teachers may not be able to make this huge mental leap in the moments required. Some of these armed teachers may have seen this child grow up from the earliest of grade levels to the point now where this child has brought a firearm to school. Some teachers may not be able to wrap their minds around the fact that this child has transitioned from student to killer. The question for all educators and school administrators is will any of their armed teachers use deadly force against children to save themselves and others from being killed?

For any armed teacher to hesitate in taking lethal action against a student who has transitioned to killer only adds a false sense of security and more danger to an already volatile situation and places everyone in greater danger. If the educator has any doubt, he or she should not be armed!

Schools are spending thousands of dollars constructing or retrofitting their front doors with a *single point of entry*. Hardening only the front door of the school requires any guest (or potential shooter) to walk into the "designated and fortified" area and be granted or denied entry through a set of doors all designed to restrict entrance. These construction projects offer a false sense of security to make people think this will truly stop the school shooter entering the school. It is almost as if they are expecting school shooters to be polite enough to enter—or attempt to enter—only through this entrance, and when entry is denied, they will just give up and go away. In fact, there are many entrances to access the school grounds, many of them are not through the front door of the school. All one really has to do is to watch students as they enter their school to see how they gain access via open gates and through the sides or rear doors. In reality, school shooters will not always enter through the front door. Many of the school shooters are students themselves or invited guests who are already inside the school or allowed access inside the school along with their concealed firearms.

On April 11, 2017, a man appeared at a school in San Bernardino, California, where his estranged wife worked. The man gained entrance via the front office and went directly to the classroom where his wife taught. The man produced a firearm and shot his wife and one special-needs student. After those two deaths, the man shot and killed himself.

Another vulnerability of the single point of entry is the bullet-resistant glass window leading into the office area. The glass may offer some security if the shooter fires directly into the glass, but the walls surrounding this window has no fortification and uses regular drywall which offers no protection from rounds that may be fired into the wall. Also, the exterior windows adjacent to the front doors consist of just regular glass and not bullet-resistant. If the shooter elected to, he/she can just break and step through the empty window frame and into any classroom and subsequently have access to the entire school.

Regarding special events, since the October 1, 2017, shooting in Las Vegas, Nevada, that claimed fifty-nine lives, many concerts, special events, and professional sports venues have utilized a screening system at their points of entry. Numerous venues screen their attendees via a walk-through metal detector and handheld metal detectors. Many of these events have heavily armed uniformed law enforcement officers stationed throughout the events grounds as a deterrence.

However, some of the events seem to fall short of overt law enforcement presence. I attended a concert in Sacramento, California, where a huge line of people waiting to be screened to get into the front door took approximately thirty minutes. During this period, I did not notice the presence of any law enforcement officers among the crowd who might be on the lookout for threats among the concertgoers.

In my opinion, this leaves everyone in the screening line extremely vulnerable to an active shooter, assailant, or any other threat to personal safety. I was also told there were no provisions whatsoever for the storage of firearms for off-duty or retired law enforcement officers to take their weapons inside the event and check their weapons once inside the venue.

One strategy that could be used is for these venues to recruit and permit armed off-duty and retired law enforcement personnel to attend their events. These off-duty and retired officers would simply meet in the security office one to two hours prior to the scheduled time of the doors opening.

All personnel would have a face-to-face with other armed law enforcement officers attending the event, notice clothing descriptions, place their ticketed seating locations on a master seating chart, and be issued a banner to be used only in cases of emergency. The banner (previously illustrated as the Don't Shoot Me banner) could be given to each plainclothes off-duty and retired officer attending that venue's event. If there was an active shooting during the time these personnel were attending the event, each officer could utilize a banner and become a force multiplier until relieved by on-duty personnel.

Active Shooter Defense Errors

Active shooter defense training can be summed up with sixteen deadly errors to be avoided. Committing one or more of these errors can have a significant effect on the chances of surviving an active shooter event either for the individual or the persons inside any organization.

#1:   Failure to conduct suitable active shooter defense training

After the 2007 Virginia Tech Virginia active shooting where thirty-two people were killed, a host of civilian and police trainers flooded the market with their brand of training. The actual qualifications of the trainers range from highly qualified individuals to those who gained their knowledge only over the internet after reading about active shootings. Many company and corporate trainers are quick to parrot *run, hide, fight* but have no real concept on how to do any of these effectively. As for the fight portion of their phrase, there are more instructions (directions) on using a bottle of shampoo than there is specificity from these so-called knowledgeable instructors on how to effectively fight or disarm an active shooter/assailant.

Potential victims of an active shooter (who are there from the moment the first shot was fired) need to know what they can do to stay alive during an active shooting. The bottom line is <u>people need to know how to properly ambush the shooter to</u> **disarm and disable** <u>him or her should they come face-to-face with the shooter or if the shooter breaches their concealed location.</u>

There are law enforcement agencies who provide active shooter training to a business or school, but in reality, what these agencies did was conduct a "tactical exercise" mainly for the benefit of their own law enforcement personnel. In these acts of purported training, the agency provides a scenario where a role-player is the shooter inside the business or school.

Civilians from that environment are recruited to play a part in the training by dressing and acting as victims of the shooter. The role-playing victims are staged throughout the crisis area displaying a myriad of trauma and simulated gunshot wounds or are sheltered in a locked and barricaded room. The law enforcement tactical personnel then conduct their training exercise as they move throughout the facility to locate the shooter, firing paintballs or rubber bullets. In some cases, blanks are fired from police weapons to provide the noise and almost add realism to the training.

Civilians who have participated in this type of "training" walk away feeling more traumatized than educated about what they themselves could or should do during an active shooting. This type of training may work for law enforcement tactical personnel but does *nothing* for civilians other than to make them even more dependent on a law enforcement response.

This type of training emphasizes and reinforces that police will respond to an active shooter and everyone should just get down and out of their way to allow the shooter to be located and neutralized by law enforcement. Law enforcement needs to remember that it is these (mostly unarmed) citizens who are inside the kill zone with an armed person who is actively stalking and killing as many people as possible from the onset of the attack while law enforcement officers are still responding to the location.

Any person who may experience an active shooter needs to know what to do, how and when to do whatever it takes to survive the shooting until one of three things occur: (1) the people inside that environment neutralize the shooter; (2) the shooter stops his or her own aggression; (3) law enforcement respond, locate, and quickly neutralize the shooter/assailant.

A large number of Schools conduct "lockdown" or "Code Red

drills." These are drills where the school administrator announces over the school's public address system. Once the drill is announced, all teachers follow their school protocol where classroom doors are locked, lights turned off and children are kept quiet until the drill has been concluded minutes later.

The most significant problems with these types of drills are as follows: The teachers within the school are not advised of the "Code Red" drill until surprised by the announcement that day. These drills are typically conducted during the most convenient times of the school day, times when students are known to be inside their respective classrooms. What happens to the students who have left the classroom for one reason or another (restroom, enroute to or from the nurse's office, etc.) One would assume the time chosen for the lockdown drill makes it easy to account for each child and allows the administrator to "check the box" the drill has been completed successfully. One question to ask is what would happen if a "real Code Red" was called when the children are outside of their classrooms. Children need to be taught what to do if an active shooter strikes when they are outside of their classrooms. Administrators should give serious thought to their protocol if it was needed at other times of the day: the very beginning of school day, during the various lunch periods and at the end of school day when the children have left the purported safety of their respective classrooms.

Once a "lockdown drill" has been conducted (or a real lockdown has occurred) school personnel are never advised or debriefed as to the results of the drill, what went right, what went wrong and how they can improve. Without crucial feedback, school personnel will continue to do what they did during the last "lockdown" whether it was the right or wrong response.

On several occasions I have given active shooter defense presentations to high ranking members a major school district only to be met with arrogant ignorance. This same school district has experienced four highly publicized school shootings and yet as of this writing, this same school district has not provided one iota of training to their members on what to do when gunshots are fired other than hide and keep quiet. A number of educators from this district have privately attended my active shooter defense training sessions by happenstance are were astonished to discover their School district has not made my training available to the district. That same school district needs to stop playing politics due to their passive and naive narrative and provide school personnel with the training and tools to save every child's and adult's life entrusted to them.

Other types of training for businesses can be in the form of "table-top exercises." This type of training is conducted solely in a classroom setting where participants are presented with a scenario and the trainer goes around the room to call on individuals who from their seated positions report what actions they would take in the scenario. I have attended numerous table-top exercises during my career, only to repeatedly see this type of training does not provide the attendees what they really should or could do to protect themselves against the threat of an active shooter. This type of training is designed to make the participants feel good about themselves, but fails to give concrete tactics and techniques they can use when the gunshots are fired.

At the conclusion of the training, Instructors ask participants to complete evaluations to rate the class. Active shooter defense training should be evaluated and rated by providing answers to the following questions: Did the training cover specific lifesaving measures? Did the students practice specific and practical techniques and tactics they could use to save their own lives? Or, was the training something that appeared to be put together just to check the box so that the entity/ organization could say they conducted training? Organizations should never be allowed to conduct active shooter training by merely watching a short video or taking a brief yearly online course.

Suitable training should address all the issues raised and more. At the end of the day, when training is over, students should have been provided with specifics as to what happens when shots are fired in their presence and what options (other than hiding in a closet or under a desk) they can use to save their lives. All participants should be educated and empowered to take the necessary actions to save their own lives and not just depend on law enforcement response when there are viable options available whether the event occurs in their workplace or elsewhere.

Seek and participate in training on bleeding control in the event you may need to treat others (or yourself) for a gunshot wound. Once law enforcement arrives to an active shooter scene, they will have to clear the building and area of any threats. This could take from minutes to hours before they deem the building safe from additional threats.

If you or another person may be gravely injured, knowing how to control the bleeding can be the difference between life and death. The training provides the use of tourniquets, direct pressure, or other measure may be required to save one or more lives until emergency medical help arrives. This type of training is usually made available through your local ambulance company or hospital.

#2:   Bureaucratic paralysis

This occurs when, through nonsensical policies, people in key leadership positions hinder or prohibit law-abiding citizens from properly defending themselves against a deadly threat. One thing that is overlooked are the hundreds of retired law enforcement personnel all over the United States. Under the federal Law Enforcement Safe Act (LEOSA) these retired officers may carry a concealed firearm in every state and across state lines.

These officers, once retired from their law enforcement careers, often go on to work in other jobs outside of the law enforcement field. These retired officers should be sought out, recruited, and appreciated for their talents, skills, and survival abilities. Once these personnel are in employed in other jobs, or as volunteers, they can use their unique skills to protect those within their worksite, but not if they are refused the legal right to have in their possession the firearms they have been trained to use over the course of their prior law enforcement careers.

#3:   Lack of situational awareness

It is imperative that you are fully and mentally present while in public. Limit electronic distractions such as having earbuds or headphones affecting both ears. Another distraction is the obsession with using smartphones or tablets where the user is totally engrossed on the device screen and unable to notice environmental dangers. When in public, be capable of using your senses (sound and sight) to notice the environment around you in case you need to take action for your own safety.

#4:   Failure to recognize danger signs

Take note of things in your environment that should or should not be there. In the 2007 Virginia Tech shooting, the perpetrator has placed chains and padlocks on the doors to keep his potential victims from escaping or law enforcement from entering. Is there a person entering or already inside a facility carrying a large duffel bag or backpack? Are one or more people dressed oddly or wearing anything unusual?

In the 2011 Arizona shooting of Gabrielle Giffords, the shooter approached the scene wearing earplugs in his ears to protect his hearing from the loud gunshots. The Aurora, Colorado revealed the shooter wearing ballistic-type attire. Is there a person who is armed that should not be?

Also, what should be there but is missing? Should there be a receptionist who is normally seated at the front of an access area, or security posted there, or patrolling inside a business or building and for some unknown reason they are not there? Is there the absence of the usual security measures that would normally be present but is not? Are there doors that should be secured and locked but are open and unlocked? Take immediate action when you first notice danger signs.

You may only have a few moments before things completely unravel and danger reveals itself.

#5: Inability to notice the armed person

Oftentimes, an active shooter has entered a facility with their firearm already in their hands. The only people who might possibly have an unholstered handgun in their hands would be law enforcement officers (on-duty, off-duty, plainclothes detectives) involved in the official performance of their duties and while they are in the presence of imminent danger. Other armed persons could be a Good Samaritan who may be acting upon seeing the presence of imminent danger that perhaps you failed to see. If those options are not the case, consider the armed person might just be a person with the intent of inflicting harm upon innocent people. And in all cases, should you see a person in regular clothing or dressed in tactical gear <u>with no law enforcement markings armed with any type of weapon</u> (handgun or long gun) take immediate action to ensure your safety. The first option is to leave the entire area and summon law enforcement once you are safe. The second option is to be prepared to save your life using other measures listed in this guide.

#6: Mistaking gunshots for other sounds

Some people who were present at the scene of shootings describe the initial sounds of gunshots as books hitting a hard surface, loud popping sounds, or booms. Some have described the sounds as fireworks, while others thought the gunshots were sounds of hammering or construction. If you don't know what gunshots sound like, visit a firearms range to learn what they sound like. There is a distinction in sounds between smaller caliber firearms and larger caliber firearms. There are also differences as to the sound when gunshots are inside a building versus outside. Every person should know what gunshots sound like and not confuse them with anything else.

The firing of blanks for familiarization purposes during training should occur only with the permission and/or assistance of local law enforcement. If any trainer fires blanks during training without law enforcement knowledge, someone within earshot not aware of the training may hear "shots fired" and summon law enforcement. Have law enforcement involved in the training if you elect to fire blanks will prevent unnecessary calls to 9-1-1 prompting a law enforcement response, not to mention the potential of a friendly fire accident where the person firing blanks is mistaken for a real active shooter.

Adults should be the only participants to experience training exercises where the firing of blanks for familiarization is conducted. <u>Under no circumstances should children be present when blanks are fired as it may have the effect of inducing trauma into their lives</u>. Firing of blanks for gunshot familiarization should be communicated well in advance so that all the adults will know it is only an exercise for their benefit. Otherwise, firing blanks in any type of civilian training environment should never be conducted.

Lastly, should you elect to include the firing of blanks in your training for familiarization, this training should never come as a surprise. Everyone involved in the training should know the exact date and time of the training. This prevents anyone confusing the firing of blanks for familiarization with an actual active shooting.

#7:   Neglecting signs of commotion

The sights and sounds of people running or screaming and the sounds of furniture being toppled over or glass breaking are obvious sounds of some type of commotion. Whenever you notice signs of commotion, it is in your best interest to determine whether the commotion is a threat to your safety and if so, take immediate action. Your immediate action should be to escape to a place of safety, not to go to the source or location to investigate the cause of the commotion.

#8:   Improper responses of fight, flight, or freeze

When danger signs of an active shooter/assailant are occurring (whether shots have been fired or not) and those who are present fail to respond properly, those few moments wasted can make the difference between life and death. Only the situation can dictate which of the two responses (fight or flight) is most appropriate. Never become the deer in the headlights and freeze in place.

Two other examples of doing the wrong thing at the wrong time stem from the Las Vegas, Nevada shooting on October 1, 2017. Video and photographs illustrate several concert participants who chose to impede their running from the shooter by using their cell phones to film their own and others escape from the concert. Another example is when one concert participant elected to demonstrate his act of defiance and stand high above the crowd as he flipped off the shooter. Know that as each precious second ticks by, your options for survival diminish. You must be fully aware of all your options for survival to *take immediate action* for your best chance of survival.

#9:   Failure to act

This refers to the mind-set of leadership who prefer to remain arrogantly ignorant to the potential of an active shooter coming to their workplace, house of worship, school, or a place of recreation. These people think and act as if it could never happen in their environment and refusing to take steps to mitigate the shooting. When danger is obviously present (in the immediate or not too distant future) the person or persons in charge should take assertive steps to make or keep the environment safe for everyone.

This is not the time for leadership to stick their collective heads in the sand to ignore, downplay, or fail to address the threat (real or perceived). Individuals who fail to act and fail to protect those whom they have supervision over can and have been held liable for huge financial judgements in subsequent civil matters.

Leaders of every organization should realize that active shooters might be attracted to their location for any number of reasons. All leaders should have a sense of responsibility and duty to protect those within the environment they have control over. Therefore, having adequately trained and/or armed personnel immediately present to launch an effective counterattack against an active shooter should be an essential element of their mission.

Establish a threat assessment team to assess potential violent threats. The team would meet within the guidelines established by each organization. Whenever the team convenes, it is to determine if the person purported to be the threat within their environment, presents or poses such a threat to the lives and safety of one more persons, that immediate actions criminal and/or civil measures should be taken to mitigate the threat.

#10: Being unaware of your exits and environment

Whether you are inside your workplace, house of worship, school, sporting event, concert, restaurant, shopping mall and a host of public places, know where several exits are and places you may need to move to seek help expeditiously. Also determine where there are places you may be able to temporarily hide to launch a counterattack. Those places should facilitate your ambush of the shooter should that person breach your location.

#11: Improper use of cover

In present-day times, some trainers still teach adults to hide under a desk, table or hide in an enclosed space from an active shooter. One definition of insanity is repeatedly doing the same thing and expecting different results. While I do understand the desperation to place something between you and a person firing a weapon indiscriminately, be cognizant of choosing an enclosed space to hide inside where you cannot fight back, or staying there in one spot too long may place you at the mercy of the shooter. Instead, the desk, church pew or other piece of furniture you are using for cover should be only be used as temporary cover until a better option is available, an all-out escape if available, and always be prepared to ambush the shooter.

#12:   Failure to learn and practice last-resort techniques

There are techniques especially designed to **disarm and disable** an armed person in an expeditious manner. Everyone who feels they even remotely someday be in any environment with an active shooter should take the time to learn and practice these techniques. Learn how to disarm a person armed with a handgun, long gun or edged weapon and practice each technique often. These are perishable skills that need to be practiced regularly.

Failing to practice these techniques on a regular basis may impact the defender being capable of successfully using them when they are needed the most. The adage of if you don't use them, you will lose them most definitely apply to these skills.

#13:   Failure to have the proper equipment

If you have taken the time and expense of obtaining a concealed firearm license, please carry a caliber of firearm that has significant knockdown power. In the unlikely event that you may engage a shooter, if any of your rounds hit their intended target, the results you are looking for is to stop the shooter from killing you or others.

Carry your licensed and concealed firearm everywhere you can legally carry the weapon. Active shooters know that soft targets are the places that have signage, policies or practices that either prohibit or restrict weapons on that property. Have your weapon on your person and in a secure holster at all times that you are out in public, unless the environment forbids you under penalty of arrest should you be discovered with a concealed firearm on that premises.

Never carry a concealed handgun in a purse or backpack. If a thief were to steal the purse or backpack, the concealed handgun inside that stolen item is also lost, as is the ability to defend yourself against a deadly attack by the thief or a shooter. There are shoulder slings that keep the pack close to the chest or belly bands keeping the handgun around your torso. Closely investigate any holster you might use before purchasing and using the item.

Leaving your handgun in a vehicle may also run the risk of your vehicle being burglarized and your handgun stolen. Once a thief steals the handgun you may be left without something you may need in the immediate or not too distant future. Not to mention that your previously owned handgun is now in the hands of some unknown criminal who is more than likely to commit a violent crime using your handgun. You can install a handgun safe that is bolted to the floor of the vehicle and out of plain sight to be used only for temporary storage of your handgun.

Always carry additional ammunition in the event you may need to fire more than the first volley of shots at the shooter or shooters. You should be very familiar with all your holsters for both your firearm and ammunition.

When drawing your handgun, it should never be in a quick draw fashion. When you observe the deadly threat, remove your handgun calmly and smoothly as you have practiced hundreds of times at the firing range and properly address the threat. Know that smooth is quick.

If you are in low-light conditions (such as a movie theater), carry a tactical LED flashlight with sufficient lumen to illuminate the area with light.

Keep your cell phone charged with the highest percentage of available battery life remaining. There are portable charging devices that you can keep with you to recharge your cell phone battery in the event it runs down. Unless otherwise needed, keep your phone silenced to prevent you from forgetting to silencing it if a real need occurs.

#14: Failure to recognize, engage, and exploit the shooter's weaknesses

You should never yell at, challenge or engage an active shooter in conversation of any kind. When a shooter has a firearm in their possession and prepared to use it, this is the time for action and not negotiations. In a significant amount of active shooting cases, it is later revealed that the shooter's weapon had run out of ammunition and the shooter took the time to reload. Other cases illustrated the shooter's weapon malfunctioned causing them to transition to a different weapon (another firearm or an edged weapon).

Use any break in the shooting to your advantage to determine when to launch a counterattack while the shooter is not ready! <u>Take advantage of the shooter when they are attempting to clear their malfunctioning weapon, reloading, or transitioning to another weapon</u>. This may be the one and only chance you have to exploit the shooter and launch a successful counterattack aimed at either shooting, disarming or disabling the shooter.

While I do acknowledge the fear that can impact an individual before or during an active shooting, they must participate and take part in their own survival. Shooters cannot see 360 degrees around them and at all times. Locate and attack the shooter in their blind spot.

There are past shootings where a person who was legally carrying their concealed handgun and in the immediate area when the killer appeared to begin their rampage. The legally armed defender saw the killer but did not to engage the shooter for whatever reason. If you are licensed to carry a concealed handgun, and you are present to see an active shooter approach, begin or continue to kill people, and you have the competence coupled with the confidence with your firearm, <u>engage using lethal force and neutralize the shooter</u>, regardless of the shooter's weapon. You may just make the difference between only a few casualties or a complete massacre. If the shooter is wearing body armor, be prepared to deliver accurate fire to other viable targets on the shooter's body or head to stop him or her.

#15: Reluctance to use deadly force

Regardless of the identity of the shooter, whether the shooter is an adult male, female, a young child or adolescent, any person who has the capacity to use deadly force to stop the shooter but is reluctant for whatever reason will not tip the balance of safety in their favor, but maintain the unstable and deadly environment.

During the February 14, 2018 Parkland, Florida, shooting, there was an on-duty armed law enforcement officer at the school while the shooter was still involved in his rampage, and for whatever the reason, the law enforcement officer failed to enter the building to engage the shooter. The hesitation on the part of any armed defender to intervene will allow the shooter to continue to kill many people within that environment. Most active shooters will stop killing innocent people when they are successfully or lethally engaged from a competent defending source whether armed or unarmed.

There is no such thing as a fair fight with an active shooter! When defending yourself, you are not required to have a face to face with the active shooter. Consider rather than taking the shooter on face to face, it is recommended to use any force necessary and without warning or when the shooter cannot see you. This may entail launching a counterattack from the rear of the shooter where you surprise him/her.

Do not attempt to take the active shooter into custody or give verbal warnings to drop their weapon. This may work in movies, but I would never recommend doing this in real life. Giving the shooter verbal commands to stop their deadly actions could be answered by the shooter firing a volley of bullets in your direction preventing you from defending yourself. The shooter has already demonstrated he/she has and will continue to kill. When you are acting to protect yourself (and others) from such deadly force, no verbal warning is required.

#16:   Failure to prepare for the arrival of law enforcement

An active shooter/assailant is <u>a person or persons *actively* engaged in the act of shooting, killing, has killed or attempting to kill innocent people</u>. These killers have used a host of weapons, from firearms of all kinds to edged weapons and vehicles during their rampage to kill as many people as possible.

If you are in the process of defending or have defended yourself against an active shooter/assailant, know that someone more than likely has summoned law enforcement and their arrival may be at any moment. If you are using a concealed handgun or have disarmed the shooter of their firearm, once law enforcement does arrive, they may be incapable of immediately distinguishing the good guys from the bad guys.

Even though you may have survived the murderous attack from the shooter, you must also take assertive steps to ensure responding law enforcement does not mistake you for the bad guy. All law enforcement agencies may operate with a different set of tactics on how they respond to an active shooter. Do not expect law enforcement to issue verbal commands to any person holding a firearm. All that may be known by the time of law enforcement's arrival is that shots were fired and when they arrive, anyone in possession of a firearm may be the person who fired those shots. Having a firearm in your hands when law enforcement arrives will only increase your chance of being seen as "the shooter" and not the good guy. As quickly as you took action to engage the shooter (whether you took action with your concealed handgun or disarmed the shooter of their weapon) you must get the weapon out of your hands just as quickly.

This is the time you may be at grave risk of being shot by friendly fire. You may be seen as the shooter by either law enforcement or from another person who may have a concealed weapon and is attempting to intervene against who they perceive as the shooter.

It is for these reasons that if you have the availability of communicating with the 9-1-1 operator, tell the 9-1-1 operator what is going on, your exact location and include your physical description as well as your clothing. Describe your ethnicity, and your gender. If you are still engaged in defending yourself, especially when using a firearm, ensure you inform the 9-1-1 operator of the type of weapon you are using and if your location changes inside that environment. If you know of the type of weapon the active shooter is using, provide that information as well.

I will cover additional information later in Part Three; Using a concealed firearm (handgun) where I provide tactics for the best and worst-case scenarios.

As discussed in my last publication, Shots Fired, I created a unique identifier concept for retired law enforcement personnel to use in the event they have drawn their concealed firearms and take lethal action against an active shooter or other deadly force threat. Since Shots Fired was published, I have met with many retired law enforcement officers from police and sheriff departments throughout the West Coast. Every one of them expressed their desire to continue to help and need to use the unique identifier to keep them from being shot by friendly fire. This is where a fraternal order of police, police unions, sheriff associations, and all representatives of the agencies they retired from need to apply subtle pressure to their respective organization's leadership to endorse this concept.

Dispatch personnel in every agency can easily compile a list of retired off-duty personnel and assign their unique identifier. When retired personnel apply for their initial or recurrent LEOSA qualification, the number can be boldly printed on their LEOSA card. The information on the card (name and photo of the retired sworn officer) can also be placed in their respective law enforcement dispatch data bank for future reference.

To reiterate, the unique identifier concept works as simple as this scenario:

A retired officer is assigned his identifier as R130. The "R" in the identifier designates the person is a retired sworn officer. The

130 identifies the individual retired person. Consider the following example:

> Retired Officer Johnson is having a cup of coffee at his local coffee shop when a gunman storms inside and begins shooting. Retired Officer Johnson draws his concealed handgun and shoots the gunman, who is now down on the floor. Retired Officer Johnson can use his cellular phone to call 9-1-1 and simply state the following: "This is R130. Shots fired at Mike's Coffee on First Street."

> Retired Officer Johnson can either hang up the phone and do whatever other lifesaving issues might need to be done until the arrival of any on-duty law enforcement officers, or he can stay connected to the 9-1-1 operator and provide additional details. Dispatch would immediately broadcast the following: "Shots fired at Mike's Coffee on First Street; R130 is on scene."

This unique identifier provides all responding law enforcement personnel with the immediate fact that a retired sworn officer is on scene, is most likely armed, and has taken some type of law enforcement action. All law enforcement vehicles equipped with a Mobile data computer would have that sworn officer's photograph sent via their dispatcher where these responding on-duty personnel can see the photo prior to arriving on the scene. The retired officer's photo can also be sent via cell phone text to officers responding or already on scene. Keep in mind that the photograph would be current as it was taken when the retired officer obtained his or her yearly LEOSA qualification.

When responding on-duty law enforcement personnel arrive, they should be easily able to recognize friend from foe and not endanger the life of the retired sworn officer by mistaking him or her as the active shooter, thereby reducing a friendly fire accident.

This unique identifier can also be used for all active and off-duty personnel. Each dispatch center could assign every one of their active duty-sworn personnel their own identifier that could be used if ever involved in an off-duty incident. This data base information can and should be shared with other local and regional dispatch centers in the event something occurs just outside the officer's immediate jurisdictional area.

Personal Safety Plan

Every person should know and be prepared to implement one or more of the items in this plan to save their own life or the lives of their family if they are faced with a killer bent on a deadly rampage. This plan provides options for survival which you should know and be ready to take action with at any given moment whether in a work, home or any recreational environment.

#1: Know at least two different ways to escape from an area.

#2: Determine at least two different places to hide with the intent of ambushing the shooter/assailant should he or she enter your environment. <u>Never leave a hiding place to search for the shooter.</u> If you leave your hiding place it is to find a better hiding place or to escape.

#3: Know what environmental and improvised weapons avail themselves should you need to use something to defend yourself.

#4: Know how to **disarm and disable** an active shooter in the event the shooter enters your immediate area.

#5: Determine if the people in your immediate surroundings are capable of assisting. Can they either telephone 9-1-1 or participate in ambushing the shooter/assailant if need be?

#6: Have a code word for close friends or family members when you observe an armed person or any violent act about to or currently unfolding. Use that code word to alert them to danger that is imminent. Then you and others close to you should immediately deploy lifesaving measures. In some schools, "Code Red" is the term used to indicate this threat.

#7: Have at least two different prearranged and announced family reunification areas in case family members become separated and need to be reunified within a reasonable period of time. This concept can also be used at large malls or theme parks, not exclusively used for deadly threat but also in the event you just become separated. If your cell phone unavailable, you can always meet at the designated area to rejoin separated members.

Part Three
Tactics and Techniques

....

Designated Practice Firearms

It is of critical importance when you begin to practice handgun or long gun disarms that the weapons you use during your practice sessions are 100 percent safe. Although a person experienced with handguns and long guns can ensure the weapons are unloaded and safe, it is best to *use and only practice with replica firearms as your designed practice weapons.* These weapons are not real firearms capable of actually firing using any type of gunpowder and projectile. These weapons are types of CO_2 airsoft pistols or rifles . At first glance, these weapons closely resemble real firearms in their appearance. The size and weight of these weapons actually have the look and feel of real firearms as well.

These CO_2 weapons can be purchased from most sporting goods stores. Take caution to remove any magazine from the weapon that could contain any type of BB or pellet. Wrap a brightly colored tape along numerous surfaces of the weapon and especially over the hole of the firearm barrel. This tape will serve as a quick and easy visual reminder that you are using a designated practice weapon and not the real thing.

Handgun Disarms

Techniques that are designed to disarm a handgun should consist of a two- step process. The first step is for the defender to apply one hand quickly to redirect the barrel of the handgun so that the defender is totally out of the line of fire. The second step is for the defender to add their second hand, which will actually complete the handgun disarming movement. There is always *a high probability* that in a real-life situation, any person holding a loaded handgun might actually discharge the handgun during the disarming process. The defender should never be frightened or discouraged if a round is discharged during the handgun disarm. The defender should have competently redirected the barrel of the handgun sufficiently so that the defender's body is completely out of the line of fire during that first step. Once the defender has added their second hand to complete the disarm, the shooter's handgun will be forced back toward the shooter's head or torso. If the handgun discharges at that point, ensure the shooter is the person who has been shot, not the defender performing the handgun disarm.

Defender's left hand to shooter's right gun hand

The defender will reach out with the left hand to the back of the shooter's right hand, capturing the shooter's right wrist and the back of their right hand. The defender will move the shooter's gun hand so that it is ninety degrees directly to the right and just outside the defender's torso and right arm, ensuring to be out of the line of fire of the shooter's handgun. Be careful not to move the handgun too far away in that direction. The farther the handgun is pushed away, the farther it requires the defender to reach to disarm the handgun.

The defender's right hand will reach underneath the firearm with the bottom of the fingers and top of the palm at the trigger guard to grab the right gun hand, thereby holding the shooter's firearm with two hands. The defender will point the barrel of the shooter's handgun forty-five degrees in a counterclockwise semicircular motion and toward the shooter's head.

Once the handgun barrel is facing the shooter's head, the shooter's right gun hand has been placed in a reverse wristlock position. Using the left hand to hold on to the shooter's right hand, the defender's right hand will apply the torque on the handgun by moving the shooter's right hand and weapon farther into the wristlock. The defender will push the handgun through the fingers and thumb of the shooter's right hand, thereby disarming the shooter of the handgun. When completed, the handgun should be 100 percent in the defender's right hand.

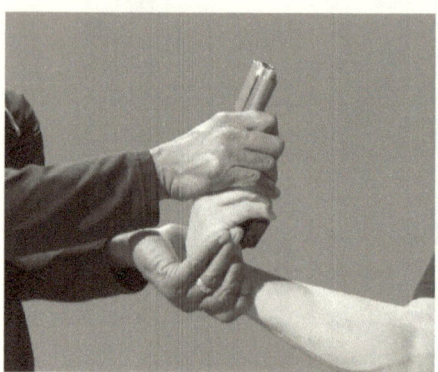 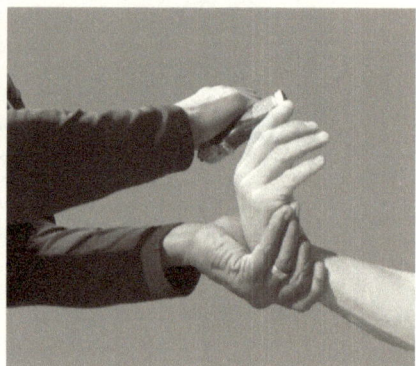

Defender's left hand to shooter's left gun hand

With the shooter holding the handgun in the left hand, the defender will reach out with the left hand to the inside palm and wrist area of the shooter's left hand. Capturing the shooter's left wrist and the inside palm portion of their left hand, the defender will move the shooter's gun hand ninety degrees directly to the right and just outside the defender's torso and right arm, ensuring to be out of the line of fire of the shooter's handgun.

The defender's right hand will reach underneath the firearm with the bottom of the fingers and top of the palm at the trigger guard to grab their left hand, thereby holding the shooter's firearm with two hands. This will allow the defender to hold on to the shooter's handgun and the shooter's left gun hand with both hands. The defender will point the barrel of the shooter's handgun directly at the shooter in a counterclockwise semicircular motion at a <u>ninety-degree</u> angle to break the shooter's left trigger finger (which may still be inside the trigger guard). Once the handgun barrel has been forced toward the shooter's torso, the handgun can be forcefully pulled away approximately twelve inches from the shooter's gun hand and ninety degrees to the defender's right effectively stripping the handgun off the trigger finger. The shooter's handgun should now be 100 percent in the defender's right hand.

Note: When practicing this technique, if the practice partner has their finger inside the trigger guard, there is a high degree of probability that the practice partner's trigger finger may be seriously injured. Therefore, <u>the practice partner should keep their trigger finger out of the trigger guard during the handgun disarming practice</u>.

If the practice partner and defender can <u>practice slowly and carefully</u>, the practice partner can keep their trigger finger inside the trigger guard. The defender must recognize when the practice partner's trigger finger is at risk of injury. The defender only needs to release the pressure on the trigger finger inside the trigger guard by reversing the rotation of the barrel away from (not towards) the practice partner. The defender should have enough slack inside the trigger guard to slowly and easily slide the weapon off the practice partner's trigger finger without injury.

When performing this technique in a real-life situation, if the shooter has their finger inside the trigger guard, the defenders' intent is to break the shooter's left trigger finger while it is still inside the trigger guard during the disarming process.

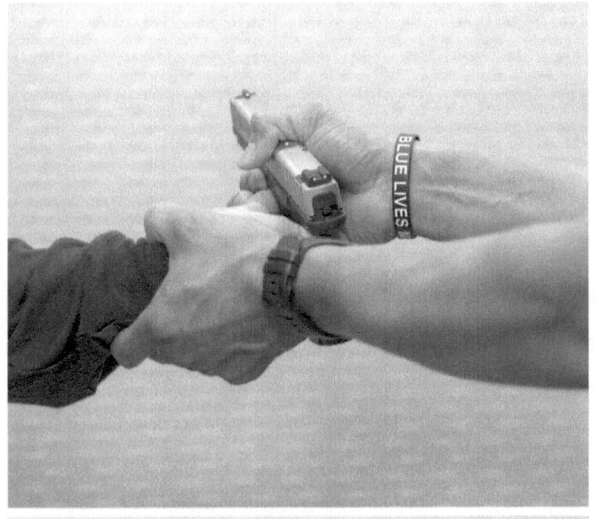

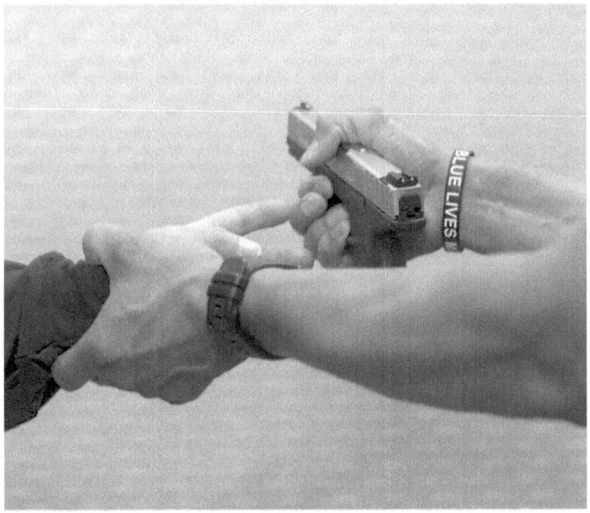

Competency on both sides

It is to the defender's advantage to be competent in disarming the shooter of their handgun regardless of in which hand the shooter is holding the weapon. There may be some situations in which the defender may be required to perform a handgun disarm where they initiate the handgun disarm with the right hand instead of the left hand. When practicing the handgun disarm techniques not illustrated by photographs, simply reverse the disarm directions using the applicable left and right along with clockwise and counter-clockwise directional technique descriptors.

Using the clock concept for positions of the shooter and defender

There are situations when the shooter will be standing directly in front of and in close proximity to the defender when the defender is the primary target. There are also situations where the shooter is standing in close proximity to the defender, but the shooter is aiming at someone else other than the defender, thereby placing the defender as a secondary target.

For the purposes of explanation, picture the face of a traditional analog clock with all the clock numbers showing from twelve at the top and moving clockwise around the clock, with the number six at the bottom of the clock.

With that clock image flat on the floor, imagine the shooter standing directly on the center of the clock face where both hands of the clock are continuously joined together. When you, the defender, are standing <u>directly in front of the shooter's firearm</u>, your position will be described as <u>standing at twelve o'clock relative to the shooter's firearm</u>. With the shooter still facing twelve o'clock, if you, the defender, are standing <u>ninety degrees to the right of the shooter's firearm (not their right shoulder) that would be the three o'clock position to the shooter's firearm</u>. With the shooter still facing twelve o'clock, if you, the defender, are standing directly behind the shooter, that would be the shooter's six o'clock position. Finally, with the shooter still facing twelve o'clock, if you, the defender, are <u>standing ninety degrees to the left of the shooter's firearm (not their left shoulder) that would be the shooter's nine o'clock position</u>. Using this concept, the following handgun disarms will apply.

Orienting yourself to the shooter and not the handgun places the defender in a more awkward position and may make the disarming technique even more unorthodox. Therefore, **orient yourself to the shooter's handgun**, not the shooter.

Moving around the shooter to various clock positions for handgun disarms

Starting with the shooter standing directly in the center of the clock where both the hands of the clock are continuously joined together, the defender will be positioned standing directly in front of the shooter at the twelve o'clock position relative to the shooter. With the shooter holding the handgun in either hand, the defender can initiate a handgun disarm with either hand, subsequently joined by the second hand to disarm the handgun completely.

With the defender moving around the clock in a clockwise direction (from the shooter's perspective), now the defender will be standing at any position between the one o'clock position and the three o'clock position. The shooter is pointing the handgun at another person who is standing at the twelve o'clock position.

For all handgun disarming techniques from the positions between the one o'clock and three o'clock positions, regardless of which hand the shooter is holding the handgun, the defender should start by standing with both feet and shoulders squarely facing and close enough to the shooter's handgun, where the defender can touch the majority of the handgun.

Initiate the handgun disarm by using their <u>left hand</u> to make the initial contact with the shooter's hand and move the gun away from both the intended victim who is standing at the twelve o'clock position as well as themselves. The defender will add the right hand and continue the handgun disarm to ensure the weapon is completely removed from the shooter's grasp.

If the defender is standing in the four o'clock through the five o'clock positions relative to the handgun, the defender must move to the three o'clock position *before* they can initiate the appropriate handgun disarm.

Note: *At no time* will defender move a shooter's handgun barrel back toward themselves. The handgun barrel will always move away from the direction of the defender at the earliest moment and expeditiously be pointed toward the shooter during the second step of the disarming process.

With the shooter holding the handgun in either hand, now the defender will be standing at any position between the eleven o'clock position and the nine o'clock position (again, relative to the handgun). The shooter is pointing the handgun at another person who is standing at the twelve o'clock position.

For all handgun disarming techniques from the positions between the eleven o'clock and nine o'clock positions, regardless of which hand the shooter is holding the handgun, the defender will initiate the disarm by using their <u>right hand</u> to make the initial contact with the shooter's hand.

The defender will move the gun away from both the intended victim who is standing at the twelve o'clock position as well as themselves. The defender will add their left hand and continue the handgun disarm to ensure the weapon is completely removed from the shooter's grasp.

If the defender is standing in the eight o'clock through the seven o'clock positions relative to the handgun, the defender must move to the nine o'clock position before they can initiate the appropriate handgun disarm.

If the defender is standing at the six o'clock position relative to the shooter, the defender can elect to move to either the three o'clock or nine o'clock position relative to the handgun and execute the appropriate handgun disarm.

Long gun disarms

Just as it was stated in the handgun disarm section, the long gun disarming technique also consists of a two-step process. The first step is for the defender to apply one hand quickly to redirect the barrel of the long gun so that the defender is totally out of the line of fire. The second step is for the defender to add their second hand over the top of the long gun close to the trigger, which will actually complete the long gun disarming movement.

Note: When the barrel of the shooter's long gun is pointed directly at the defender—and when the defender is in relatively close proximity to the shooter—the defender may use one of two options available to move out of the line of fire to initiate and complete a long gun disarm. It does not matter whether the shooter has their right hand at the trigger or their left hand at the trigger; both options have the same results.

Option #1: The defender may step with their left foot forward and in a forty-five-degree angle to their left <u>while simultaneously</u> reaching out with their right hand (palm side down) and <u>redirecting the barrel</u>

of the shooter's long gun to the right and downward in a forty-five-degree angle.

By stepping forward with the left foot at a forty-five-degree angle and simultaneously using the right hand to redirect the barrel of the shooter's long gun in a forty-five-degree angle downward and to the right, these two actions will place the shooter's long gun along the right side of the defender.

The defender will apply their left hand (also palm side down) to reach over the top of the shooter's long gun and grab the area of the long gun close to the shooter's hand near the trigger. The defender should have both hands placed firmly on the shooter's long gun palm side down to allow the maximum torque required for the disarming manipulation.

Once the defender has both hands in place, the defender will violently pull upward with their left hand (dislodging the long gun from either the torso or shoulder area of the shooter) while the defender continues to push the barrel of the long gun to the right and downward at a forty-five-degree angle.

The defender will then rotate the barrel of the long gun in a counterclockwise direction and outside of the shooter's arms until the barrel is almost in a vertical position. At this point, the barrel of the long gun can be forcefully driven into the face of the shooter. The defender will rake the barrel downward into the upper body until the long gun can be totally dislodged from the shooter's grasp.

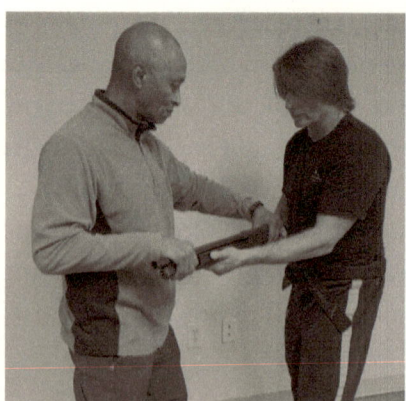

Option #2: The defender may step with their right foot forward and in a forty-five-degree angle to their right <u>while simultaneously</u> reaching out with their left hand (palm side down) and <u>redirecting the</u> <u>barrel</u> of the shooter's long gun to the left and downward in a forty-five-degree angle. By stepping forward with the right foot at a forty-five-degree angle and simultaneously using the left hand to redirect the barrel of the shooter's long gun in a forty-five-degree angle downward and to the left, these two actions will place the shooter's long gun along the left side of the defender. The defender will apply their right hand (also palm side down) to reach over the top of the long gun and grab the area of the long gun close to the shooter's hand near the trigger. The defender should have both hands placed firmly on the shooter's long gun palm side down to allow the maximum torque required for the disarming manipulation.

Once the defender has both hands firmly in place, the defender will violently pull upward with their right hand (dislodging the long gun from either the torso or shoulder area of the shooter) while the defender continues to push the barrel of the long gun downward and to the left at a forty-five-degree angle.

The defender will then rotate the barrel of the long gun in a clockwise direction and outside of the shooter's arms until the barrel is almost in a vertical position. At this point, the barrel of the long gun can be forcefully driven into the face of the shooter. The defender will rake the barrel downward into the upper body of the shooter until the long gun can be totally dislodged from the shooter's grasp.

When the shooter is pointing the long gun directly at the defender, it does not matter which option the defender uses for the long gun disarm. Once the defender has safely stepped forward at the prescribed angle <u>while simultaneously redirecting the shooter's long gun barrel</u> out of the immediate line of fire to the defender, the defender will add the second hand on top of the shooter's long gun to complete the disarm. The defender can then take one step away from the shooter and contemplate the next defensive movement should the shooter attempt to retrieve a second weapon to continue the deadly attack or charge the defender in an attempt to retrieve the disarmed long gun.

There is always a high probability that in a real-life situation, any person holding a loaded firearm might actually discharge the firearm during the disarming process. The defender should never be frightened or discouraged if a round is discharged during the firearm disarm. <u>The defender should have competently redirected the barrel of the firearm sufficiently so that the defender's body is completely out of the line of fire during the first step of the disarming process</u>. Once the defender has added their second hand to complete the disarm, the barrel of the shooter's long gun will be forced back toward the shooter's head and torso. If the weapon discharges at that point, ensure the shooter is the person who has been shot, not the defender performing the firearm disarm.

One additional issue might be the barrel of the long gun being hot to the touch, especially if the defender is performing this disarm after the shooter has been firing many rounds using this long gun. The defender should only need to hold on to the shooter's long gun barrel for a few seconds in order to complete the disarm. I would caution the defender against using gloves to prevent any type of burn to their hands. The wearing of gloves may impact the dexterity and overall ability to disarm the shooter of his or her long gun.

Moving around the shooter to various clock positions for long gun disarms

Just as in the handgun disarms, orienting yourself to the shooter and not the long gun places the defender in a more awkward position and may make the disarming technique even more unorthodox. Therefore, **orient yourself to the shooter's long gun**, not the shooter.

Starting with the shooter standing directly in the center of the clock where both hands of the clock are continuously joined together, the shooter may have either hand at the trigger. When the defender is standing directly in front of the shooter at the twelve o'clock position relative to the shooter, the defender may either use option number one (stepping with the left foot and using the right hand to redirect the barrel) or option number two (stepping with the right foot and using the left hand to redirect the barrel) to disarm the shooter of their long gun.

When the defender is standing at any position between the one o'clock position and the three o'clock position and the shooter is pointing the long gun at another person who is standing at the twelve o'clock position, the defender will initiate the long gun disarm by stepping forward directly towards the shooter with their left foot and using the right hand to make the initial contact with the shooter's long gun barrel and move the gun away from both the intended victim who is standing at the twelve o'clock position as well as themselves. The defender will add their left hand on top of and near the long gun trigger area and the shooter's hand to continue the long gun disarm and ensure the weapon is completely removed from the shooter's grasp.

If the defender is standing in the four o'clock through the six o'clock positions relative to the long gun, the defender must move to the three o'clock position (relative to the long gun) before they can complete the appropriate long gun disarm using option number one.

When the defender is standing at any position between the eleven o'clock position and the nine o'clock position and the shooter is pointing the long gun at another person who is standing at the twelve o'clock position, the defender will initiate the long gun disarm by stepping forward directly towards the shooter with their right foot and using the left hand to make the initial contact with the shooter's long gun barrel and move the gun away from both the intended victim as well as themselves. The defender will add their right hand on top and near the long gun trigger area and the shooter's hand to continue the long gun disarm and ensure the weapon is completely removed from the shooter's grasp.

If the defender is standing in the eight o'clock through the six o'clock positions relative to the long gun, the defender must move to the nine o'clock position before they can complete the appropriate long gun disarm using option number two.

Note: *At no time* will defenders move a shooter's long gun barrel back toward themselves. The long gun barrel will always move away from the direction of the intended victim and the defender at the earliest moment and the second hand added to expeditiously point the barrel toward the shooter during the disarming process.

If the defender is standing at the six o'clock position relative to the shooter, the defender can elect to move to either the three o'clock or nine o'clock position (again, relative to the long gun) and execute the appropriate long gun disarm.

Out-in-the-open tactics

One issue that is occasionally brought up during active shooter defense classes is that the firearm disarming techniques occur only when up close and personal with the armed person. The question is, what can be done to defend against a shooter who is a significant distance away and the shooter is not so easy to reach?

In most cases, active shooters will enter an area where they want to shoot and kill either a specific individual or individuals or they will begin to shoot and kill people randomly. Whenever there is a significant distance between the shooter and defender, <u>moving out of the shooter's visual line of sight and fire is the first and foremost important thing to avoid being shot</u> and provide you options for your survival.

Do what you can to move perpendicular to the shooter (moving left to right) It may be harder for the shooter to track you as opposed to moving away in a straight line to or from the shooter. If possible, move downward and out of sight of the shooter's view to a place of temporary cover or concealment.

While others may be attempting to run away from the shooter, consider that if you were to do the same thing, you might be in the rear of the group that is attempting to escape the area and perhaps adding to a bottleneck at the exit points. This moment might be the ideal time to **temporarily conceal yourself or circle around to the blind side of the shooter** with the intent to ambush him or her.

When the shooter is focused on looking or shooting in a different direction other than directly at you, this might your best time and opportunity to escape or ambush the shooter. If you chose to engage the shooter, expeditiously move toward him or her and complete what might be the single most important disarm technique to save your life and possibly the lives of others. You must **disarm and disable** the shooter to prevent him or her from transitioning to another weapon.

Ambush strategies

All ambush strategies begin with the defender out of the immediate line of sight of the shooter in order to facilitate the counterattack. Being totally out of the line of sight of the shooter can occur when either the shooter or the defender is outside an area or room or if the defender is inside the same area as the shooter, concealed from the shooter's view, or in the shooter's blind spot.

During the ambush of the shooter, do not be thrown off by the identity of the shooter. Past active shooters have been very young, old, male, female, and transgender. The shooter could even be someone you know, a family member or a person in clothing or uniform of a trusted occupation. The defender must have previously made the decision to live another day rather than die by the hand of the shooter, regardless of the shooter's identity or occupation. Hesitation on the defender's part could result in their own death and possibly the deaths of many more innocent people.

One-person ambush handgun disarm

Outside a room or area ambush tactics:

If the lone defender is on the opposite side of an area or room where a wall separates the defender from the shooter and where there is a door (or other entryway) the shooter may enter through, it is best to set up on the wall closest to the doorknob (or entry point) where you expect the shooter to enter. This position will give the defender the greatest chance of seeing the shooter before the shooter can see them.

The defender should have their back flat against the wall while anticipating the shooter to enter the area. This position will afford the defender the immediate ability of using both hand without moving far from the wall. If the defender elected to face the wall (with the abdomen close to the wall) the defender will not be afforded the immediate ability to using both hands without having to move further away from the wall before adding the second hand required for the disarm.

The defender must ensure that his or her entire body (even the feet) are concealed from the shooter. If the defender has his/her back flat against the wall, and their left hand is closest to the entry point, the defender will initiate the disarm with their left hand. If it appears there may be a considerable time before the shooter may enter that area, the defender may elect to rest onto the right knee with the back still flat against the wall. If the expected entry point is on the defender's right, the directional descriptors will be reversed.

If the defender is <u>not using an improvised weapon</u> to assist in the counterattack, as the shooter enters the area, the defender will reach forward with the hand closest to the wall and the entry point of the shooter to initiate the handgun disarm. After the shooter has been successfully disarmed, take a brief second to determine if the shooter is reaching for a second weapon to continue their deadly rampage and then take the appropriate lethal action if needed.

If the defender <u>elects to use an improvised weapon</u> to aid in their defense, the defender will disarm and disable the shooter in the following steps. As soon as the shooter enters the area, the defender will reach out with the hand closest to the wall and the shooter to push the shooter's hand holding the handgun away. The defender, holding an improvised weapon in their other hand, will then strike the shooter in the exposed area of their face or head, let go of the improvised weapon and then complete the firearm disarm.

If the defender elects to use a sharp instrument such as a pair of scissors, the first priority is to move the shooter's hand and handgun away. The second priority would be to thrust the scissors into the shooter's eyes, neck, throat, or a combination of at least two areas. If the defender uses a long bladed weapon (such as a machete or blade of a paper cutter), the weapon may be directed at the shooter's arm holding the weapon or at the shooter's neck. Once those injuries have been inflicted, the defender still needs to disarm the shooter of their weapon.

Whether using an improvised weapon to disarm a shooter or not, once the defender has disarmed the shooter of their primary firearm if the shooter begins to reach for a second deadly weapon, the defender must take immediate action, using deadly force to stop the attack. If using the shooter's firearm (or another firearm) to stop the deadly threat, shoot the attacker in areas of their body that will immediately incapacitate the shooter.

If shots are fired into the body/torso area of the shooter and the shooter does not stop, the shooter could be wearing a ballistic vest or under the influence of drugs or alcohol. The defender may need to immediately fire into another area of the shooter to stop the threat, such as the shooter's head. The defender should stop firing into the shooter when the threat has been completely neutralized.

Inside the same area as the shooter:
If the defender is in the same area of the shooter, the defender may want to stay hidden behind whatever object is temporarily concealing them from the shooter's view until he or she can make the best move to either escape or engage with the shooter. It is also critical that the defender be as quiet as possible and in control of their breathing in order not to give away their position.

When the defender moves to approach and engage the shooter, use an angle in the shooter's blind spot and where the shooter's firearm is not pointed directly at the defender. Close the distance rapidly, disarm the shooter with the appropriate handgun disarm, and disable them using the necessary force to stop any further threat.

If the defender elects to use an improvised weapon during the counterattack, remember to approach at an angle out of the shooter's view and the direction of the shooter's barrel. The priority is to redirect the shooter's barrel with one hand and then strike the shooter with the improvised weapon with the other hand. The defender can then let go of the improvised weapon and disarm the shooter of his or her handgun. After the shooter has been disarmed from their primary handgun, ensure that the shooter is disabled by using an incapacitating technique, or if justified, using lethal force.

Two-person ambush handgun disarm

As previously mentioned, all ambush strategies will begin with the defenders out of the immediate line of sight of the shooter in order to facilitate the counterattack.

Outside a room or area ambush tactics:
If the defenders are outside of an area or room where a wall separates the defenders from the shooter, they should remember to be flat against the wall. If the room has a door (or doorway) the shooter might enter through, the defenders should position themselves against the wall that is closest to the doorknob (or entryway). The defender closet to the area where the shooter may enter is designated as defender number one, and that person's job is to disarm the shooter when the shooter enters the area.

The second defender is designated as defender number two, and that person's job is to disable the shooter after defender number one disarms the shooter. Defender number two should stand with just one shoulder against that wall, directly to the rear of defender number one, and remain out of sight of the shooter. Remember, if it appears there may be a considerable time before the shooter may enter that area, the defenders may elect to rest onto one knee with the back still as flat against the wall as possible.

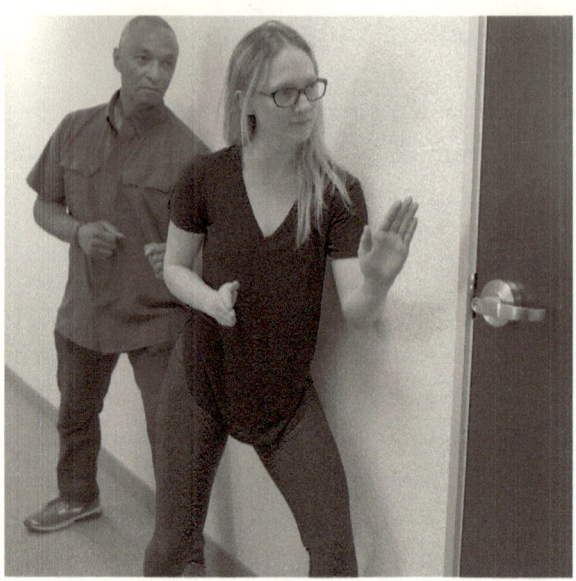

Once the shooter enters the room or area, defender number one will reach forward with the hand that is closest to the shooter's entrance area to initiate the handgun disarm. After the handgun disarm has been completed, the defender (using the hand that initiated the handgun disarm and still holding on to the shooter's gun hand) will pull the shooter further into the room or area, spinning the shooter around to expose the shooter's back to defender number two. Only after the shooter's handgun has been disarmed will defender number two will step forward and place the disarmed shooter into a carotid control hold to incapacitate the disarmed shooter. Once the carotid control hold is in place, the defender must forcefully walk the shooter backwards and force the shooter to the ground and into a seated position.

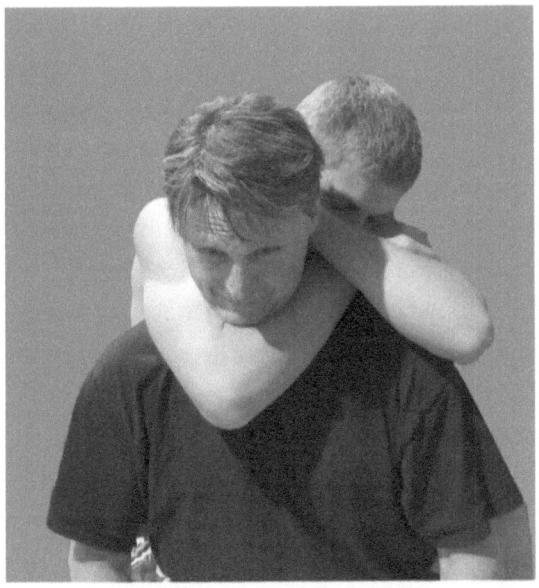

When defender number two has placed the disarmed shooter in a carotid hold, defender number one will meticulously watch the hands of the shooter to determine if the shooter is reaching for another weapon. Should the shooter touch or attempt to retrieve any additional weapons, defender number one will loudly announce the second weapon the shooter is attempting to transition to. If the weapon is a gun, defender number one will yell, "Gun!" If the weapon is a knife, defender number one will yell, "Knife!" Defender number two will immediately release the shooter from the carotid hold and quickly move away and out of the line of fire of defender number one. Defender number one may need to use the weapon he has disarmed from the shooter in order to stop continued deadly force from the shooter.

Inside the same area as the shooter:
If the defenders are in the same area of the shooter, the defenders may want to stay hidden behind whatever objects are temporarily shielding them from the shooter's view until they can make their best move to either escape or engage the shooter. It is also critical that the defenders

be as quiet as possible and in control of their breathing in order not to give away their position.

When the defender moves to approach and engage the shooter, use an angle in the shooter's blind spot and where his or her firearm is not pointed directly at the defender. Close the distance rapidly, disarm the shooter with the appropriate handgun disarm, and disable the shooter using the necessary force to stop any further threat.

If the defenders elect to use an improvised weapon, remember to consider the angle relative to the direction of the shooter's barrel. The first defender to reach the shooter will redirect the shooter's handgun barrel with one hand and strike the shooter with the improvised weapon held in their other hand. Only after the barrel of the handgun has been redirected can the shooter be disarmed. Once the shooter has been disarmed from their primary handgun, the second defender can place the shooter in a carotid control hold to incapacitating him or her.

Defender number one (who disarmed the shooter) will meticulously watch the hands of the shooter to determine if the shooter is reaching for another weapon. Should the shooter touch or attempt to retrieve any additional weapons, defender number one will loudly announce the second weapon the shooter is attempting to transition to. If the weapon is a gun, defender number one will yell, "Gun!" If the weapon is a knife, defender number one will yell, "Knife!" Defender number two (who is actively engaged in a carotid control hold with the shooter) will immediately release the shooter from the carotid control hold and quickly move away and out of the line of fire of defender number one. Defender number one may need to use the weapon disarmed from the shooter in order to stop continued deadly force from the shooter.

One-person ambush long gun disarm

Outside the room or area of the shooter:
If the lone defender is outside of an area or room where a wall separates the defender from the shooter, as previously explained, the defender must have their back flat against a wall, shielding his or her entire body and feet from the shooter. The defender should be positioned closest to the doorknob or entryway through which they anticipate the shooter will enter. The defender may use one of two strategies against the shooter. Once the shooter enters the area, the defender may elect to disarm the shooter immediately, or use an improvised weapon to initiate the counterattack before disarming the shooter. If it appears there may be a considerable time before the shooter may enter that area, the defender may elect to rest onto one knee on the ground with the back still flat against the wall. If the expected entry point is on the defender's right, the directional descriptors will be reversed.

As an example of disarming without the use of an improvised weapon, the defender has their <u>back flat against a wall</u> with their <u>left hand closest to the doorknob or entry point</u>, once the shooter enters the room exposing their long gun barrel, <u>the defender would use their right hand to grab and redirect the barrel and redirect it away.</u> The defender would then apply their left hand to the long gun at the designated place on top of the long gun nearest the trigger to complete the disarm.

For the example of using an improvised weapon before the long gun, the defender should <u>reach out with the hand closest to the wall or the entry point (the left hand)</u> to grab and redirect the long gun's barrel away from him or herself. With the improvised weapon held in the right hand of the defender, the defender can strike the shooter in the face or head. The defender should then let go of the improvised weapon, place the right hand (palm downwards) on top of the redirected barrel and left hand on top of the long gun closest to the trigger. Once both hands have been repositioned, the defender should complete the long gun disarm. Be prepared disable the shooter using the necessary force to stop any further threat.

If the defender elects to use a sharp instrument such as a pair of scissors, the first priority will always be to move the barrel of the long gun away. The second priority would be to thrust the scissors into the shooter's eyes, neck, throat or a combination of at least two areas. If the defender uses a long bladed weapon (such as a machete or school's paper cutter), the weapon may be directed at the shooter's arm holding the weapon or at the shooter's neck. Once these injuries have been inflicted, the defender still needs to disarm the shooter of their weapon.

After using the improvised weapon, the defender may then replace the hand that initially grabbed the barrel of the weapon with their other hand, placing the hand that was initially designated to grab the barrel on top of the long gun near the trigger guard and the shooter's hand to complete the long gun disarm. Although this actually adds one additional step to the disarming process, but by using the improvised weapon it will have caused significant injury to the shooter to facilitate the long gun disarm.

Inside the same area as the shooter:
If the defender is in the same area of the shooter, the defender may want to stay hidden behind whatever objects are temporarily shielding him or her from the shooter's view until he or she can make the best move to either escape or engage the shooter. It is also critical that the defender be as quiet as possible and in control of their breathing in order to avoid giving away their position.

When the defender moves to approach and engage the shooter, use an angle in the shooter's blind spot and where his or her firearm is not pointed directly at the defender. Close the distance rapidly, disarm the shooter with the appropriate long gun disarm, and disable them using the necessary force to stop any further threat.

If the defender elects to use an improvised weapon, remember to consider the angle relative to the direction of the shooter's barrel.

Redirect the shooter's barrel with one hand and strike the shooter with the improvised weapon held with the other hand. Now disarm the shooter of his or her long gun. Once the shooter has been disarmed from their long gun. Be prepared to disable the shooter using the necessary force to stop any further threat.

Two-person ambush long gun disarm

Outside the room or area of the shooter:
The defenders must be out of the immediate line of sight of the shooter in order to facilitate the counterattack. Being totally out of the line of sight of the shooter can occur when either the shooter or the defender is outside an area or room or if the defenders are concealed from the shooter's view.

Starting with the pair of defenders outside of an area or room where a wall separates the defenders from the shooter, the defender closet to the area the shooter may enter is designated as <u>defender number one</u>, and <u>their job is to disarm the shooter</u>. Defender number one must have the back flat against a wall, shielding their entire body and feet from the shooter as they anticipate the entry of the shooter into that area.

The second defender is designated as <u>defender number two</u>, and <u>their job is to disable the shooter</u> once defender number one disarms the shooter. Defender number two should stand with a shoulder against that wall and behind defender number one in the area where the shooter is expected to enter.

Defender number one has three options that can be used once the shooter enters the area. Either option is viable, however defender number one must communicate the chosen option to defender number two prior to the shooter entering the area.

<u>Option #1</u>: Completely disarm the shooter of their long gun by himself or herself. This option was previously explained in the one-person ambush long gun disarm tactics where the shooter is outside the room or area of the shooter.

Option #2: Use an improvised weapon against the shooter and disarm the shooter as the shooter enters the area without the assistance of the second defender. This option was also previously explained in the one-person ambush long gun disarm tactics where the shooter is outside the room or area of the shooter.

Option #3: Immediately cradle the shooter's long gun and allow defender number two to step in and incapacitate the shooter.

The cradle method two-person long gun disarm:
Defender number one will use both hands to reach out and underneath the shooter's long gun and cradle the shooter's long gun against their own chest. The cradle position can be obtained by the defender using both hands to reach underneath and between the shooter and the long gun. The ideal place for the defender to cradle the long gun is to grab close to the shooter's hands as he or she is holding the long gun. The defender will have placed the long gun in both hands or the inside crooks of their elbows and forearms and then will use both arms to pull the long gun tightly against their chest, ensuring the length of the long gun is held firmly against their body.

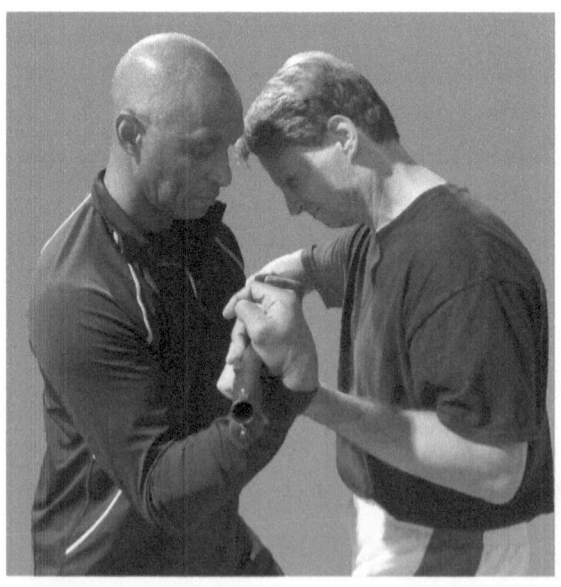

Once defender number one has successfully cradled the long gun, defender number one can control and impair the firing of the long gun and the direction of any potential shots the shooter may attempt to fire. Defender number one will then take a ninety-degree step inside the room and spin the shooter into the room to expose the shooter's back to defender number two.

Note: *At no time* will the defender ever point the shooter's long gun barrel in the direction of defender number two or another other innocent person who may be in the immediate area.

While the shooter is still holding on to the weapon and defender number one has the shooter's long gun in a cradle position, defender number two will move into position and place the shooter into a carotid control hold and render the shooter unconscious.

For the few seconds it takes for defender number two to render the shooter unconscious, defender number one must meticulously be aware of the shooter's hands to determine if the shooter is reaching for another weapon. The shooter will need to release one hand from their long gun in order to reach for a second weapon. Should the shooter reach for or touch any additional weapon, defender number one will loudly announce the second weapon the shooter is attempting to transition to. If the weapon is a gun, defender number one will yell, "Gun!" If the weapon is a knife, defender number one will yell, "Knife!"

Defender number two will immediately release the shooter from the carotid control hold and quickly move away and out of the line of fire of defender number one. Defender number one, who now notices the shooter only has one hand on the long gun should be capable of easily disarming the shooter. Defender number one will need to make the decision to use the weapon against the shooter by shooting or striking the shooter with their long gun in order to stop any continued deadly force from the shooter.

One additional issue might be that the parts of the long gun may be hot to the touch, especially if the defender is performing the cradle method after the shooter has been firing many rounds using this long gun. Defender number one should only need to hold on to the shooter's long gun for the time it takes (approximately fifteen seconds) for defender number two to use the carotid control hold and render the shooter unconscious.

Inside the same area as the shooter:
If the defenders are in the same area of the shooter, the defenders may want to stay hidden behind whatever objects are temporarily shielding them from the shooter's view until they can make their best move to either escape or engage the shooter. It is also critical that the defenders be as quiet as possible and in control of their breathing in order not to give away their positions.

When the defenders move to approach and engage the shooter, use an angle in the shooter's blind spot and where his or her firearm is not pointed directly at either defender. Close the distance rapidly, disarm the shooter with the appropriate long gun disarm, and disable them using the necessary force to stop any further threat.

If the defenders elect to use an improvised weapon, remember to consider the angle relative to the direction of the shooter's long gun barrel. The first defender to reach the shooter can redirect the shooter's long gun barrel with one hand and strike the shooter with the improvised weapon held in the other hand. Only after the barrel of the long gun has been redirected can the shooter be disarmed. Once the shooter has been disarmed from their primary long gun, the second defender can place the shooter in a carotid control hold to incapacitate him or her.

Defender number one (who disarmed the shooter) will meticulously watch the hands of the shooter to determine if the shooter is reaching for another weapon. Should the shooter touch or attempt to retrieve any additional weapons, defender number one will loudly announce the second weapon the shooter is attempting to transition to. If the weapon is a gun, defender number one will yell, "Gun!" If the weapon is a knife, defender number one will yell, "Knife." Defender number two (who is actively engaged in a carotid control hold with the shooter) will immediately release the shooter from the carotid control hold and quickly move away and out of the line of fire of defender number one. Defender number one may need to use the weapon disarmed from the shooter in order to stop continued deadly force from the shooter.

Legal possession of a concealed weapon (handgun)

Active shooters don't typically announce the day, time, and location for their deadly deeds. If you are licensed and permitted to carry a concealed handgun, keep your handgun and related tools with you in as many places as you are legally allowed to carry them.

Resist the temporary urge to leave your handgun behind and justify it by saying, "Well, I'm only going to make a quick stop and I won't need it. Besides, nothing has ever happened there before." The concealed handgun you have left behind won't do you any good if it's at your home or you left it inside your vehicle. It is always better to have your handgun with you and not need it than to need your weapon and not have it.

If you have the legal authorization to carry a concealed handgun, be careful not to break any laws that could land you in jail. Research the areas you will or might frequent to ensure you are legally allowed to carry your concealed handgun inside that environment. I personally use the following criteria to determine my legal authorization and potential for legal jeopardy:

- Is there a local, state, or federal law that prohibits me from having a lawfully concealed firearm on my person while on or inside this property?
- If I'm not allowed to have my handgun with me, does the facility have competent and armed individuals who can thwart any active shooter who may enter that venue to create mayhem?
- Are they actively screening everyone who enters their property, area, or event using a walk-through metal detector, hand wand, or physical search (pat down)? Going into a facility and being flagged carrying a legally concealed firearm would just draw attention to myself and possibly a distraction from anyone carrying an illegally concealed firearm.

If any of the three criteria will not allow me to carry my legally concealed firearm on my person, I will have to make the choice to secure it elsewhere, or not enter the premises.

Some private businesses indicate by way of signage or their policy prohibit weapons on their property or inside their facility, stating or otherwise indicating it is a gun-free zone. Those types of places usually have <u>more of a company policy than a law</u>. If you are legally authorized to carry a concealed firearm in that type of situation and someone notices your concealed weapon, they might advise you of their policy and ask you to leave. If that establishment is not conducive to having legally armed citizens carrying their concealed weapons (who would more than likely be the ones to defend themselves on or in the premises) I would personally prefer to go elsewhere.

Using a concealed firearm (handgun)

If the need arises and you must take action to save your life (and perhaps the lives of others immediately in your vicinity), decide on the best time to draw your handgun to shoot the active shooter who is, has, or about to be involved in the act of killing innocent people. **Make sure you are 100% certain that the person you are about to fire on is the active shooter and not a legally armed citizen who may have prematurely drawn their weapon in their attempt to defend themselves.**

When you draw your handgun, it should never be in a quick draw fashion. The drawing of your handgun is a movement you have practiced hundreds of times before this critical moment. When drawing your concealed handgun, either draw while moving perpendicular to the shooter, or from a position that affords cover and concealment, or when the shooter is not looking in your direction.

Removing the handgun from your holster should be careful and deliberate, ensuring your safety and the lives of other innocent people around you. Never allow your adrenalin to overcome you to the point where you are not in complete control of your own physical movements.

Ensure that you are physically and mentally prepared to use deadly force to stop the shooter. Do not fire your weapon until you have positive identification of the active shooter and can place accurate rounds on the intended target, the shooter.

From the December 29, 2019 West Freeway Church shooting in Texas, one of the armed security team members drew his firearm on the active shooter. The armed security team member fired one shot to neutralize the shooter. The time elapsed from when the shooter produced and fired his first round until the armed security member drew and fired his concealed firearm to neutralize the suspect was six seconds.

Remember that shooters can be of any ethnicity, age, gender and occupation. Do not be surprised to see the shooter represent any of these categories.

In the event you have drawn your handgun or disarmed the shooter of their firearm, keep in mind that there could possibly be more than one shooter/assailant. Be cognizant of all those around you to ensure your safety. One compelling reason to escape from the entire area immediately is not only because it has been determined as a kill zone but because there could also be additional shooters/assailants, or they could have added potential explosive devices to the area.

If you have fired shots at the active shooter there are a number of items that you may want to do next. Starting with the best-case scenarios and moving to the worst case, let's discuss these items. Keep in mind, these are just some of the highlights of a whole host of items you may need to perform.

BEST CASE: You <u>fired on the shooter with your handgun the shooter is down</u> and no longer a threat.

- Take cover (if cover is available) and immediately ascertain if there is another shooter in the immediate area.
- If you need to reload, do so.
- Holster and conceal your loaded handgun.
- If you can leave the immediate area, go to a safer place and call 9-1-1.
- Advise the 9-1-1 operator you were involved in a shooting with the suspect and what you believe is the shooter's location and extent of injuries.
- Advise the 9-1-1 operator your present location, your identity and physical description (including clothing).
- Advise the 9-1-1 operator that you are armed with your weapon holstered and that you will wait for law enforcement to arrive with your hands empty and in plain sight.
- Follow all the directions of the 9-1-1 operator and more importantly, the arriving law enforcement personnel!

- Arriving law enforcement personnel will not know the full story of what has transpired, and they will follow their protocol.
- Officers may treat you as a "suspect" until they can establish you acted as one of the good guys.

BEST CASE: You are <u>unarmed and have physically engaged the active shooter.</u>

- You are either close enough to the shooter to touch him or her, or you have concealed yourself in a position to ambush him or her once they enter your location.
- After you have disarmed the shooter of their firearm (handgun or long gun), the shooter attempts to transition to a second weapon (handgun or knife) in their waistband.
- Seeing the shooter reach for that second weapon, you elect to use the weapon you disarmed from the shooter to shoot him/her.
- Fire only the number of rounds into the shooter to "stop the threat."
- The shooter falls to the ground due to the injury you just inflicted using the shooter's firearm.
- Immediately determine if there is a second active shooter in your immediate area.
- If you face no threat from a second shooter, move away from the shooter into the shooter's blind spot and take cover where you can observe his/her immediate actions.
- You are in a unique situation where the shooter has been disarmed, you are not going to render aid to him/her, but need to ensure he/she does not move from that position to pose a deadly threat to any other person.
- Place the shooter's weapon on the ground, but within arms reach while you summon the 9-1-1 operator to advise of what has transpired.

- <u>Do not hold the shooter's weapon in your hand when you believe that law enforcement will arrive shortly.</u>
- Advise the 9-1-1 operator you were involved in a shooting with the suspect after disarming the shooter of their firearm, your exact location and what you believe is the extent of the shooter's injuries.
- Advise the 9-1-1 operator of your identity and physical description (including clothing).
- Advise the 9-1-1 operator that you disarmed the shooter of his/her weapon and you have placed that weapon on the ground.
- Inform the 9-1-1 operator that you will wait for law enforcement to arrive with your hands empty and in plain sight.
- Remember that law enforcement will be unable to initially differentiate the good guy from the bad guy.
- Follow the directions of law enforcement personnel.
- Officers may treat you as a "suspect" until they can establish you acted as one of the good guys.

WORST CASE: You fired on the shooter using your handgun and <u>the shooter is not down and still represents a threat</u>!

- Take cover and keep your weapon ready should the shooter further reveal himself/herself.
- Be aware of your weapon and reload when the situation dictates.
- Immediately determine if you are in the best cover position, or if you need to move to another place that offers better cover, or if you should attempt to escape from the area.
- Ascertain if there are other shooters in the immediate area.
- If you can leave the immediate area, go to a safer place and call 9-1-1.
- If you are not able to leave your position, and you can call 9-1-1, advise the 9-1-1 operator you are involved in a shooting with

the suspect(s) and what you believe is the shooter or shooters locations.

- Advise the 9-1-1 operator your exact location and physical description to include clothing. REPEAT YOUR PHYSICAL AND CLOTHING DESCRIPTION
- If you have seen the shooter, advised the 9-1-1 operator of the suspect's description.
- Advise the type of weapon you are using and (if know) the type of weapon the suspect is using (handgun, shotgun, semi-automatic rifle).
- If you are using a cellular telephone, use your handsfree Bluetooth device. If you are not using a blue tooth (hands free device) and unable to hold the cell phone, lay the phone down close to you and place it on speaker if you can keep the 9-1-1 operator on the open line.
- Advise the 9-1-1 operator (once you are safe to do so) you will wait for law enforcement to arrive and surrender yourself and your position to them, especially if you are still engaged in a firefight.
- If you are injured, advise the extent of your injuries.
- If you know of others that are injured, the 9-1-1 operator may request to know that information.
- Follow all the directions of the 9-1-1 operator and more importantly, the arriving law enforcement personnel.
- Arriving law enforcement personnel will not know the full story of what had transpired so they will follow their protocol.
- Officers may treat you as a "suspect" until they can establish you acted as one of the good guys.

Armed shielding concept

Should you need to draw your handgun and need to move from a dangerous location when you have a loved one with you, or you may need to escort an innocent person out of a dangerous environment, there is a technique you can use as you protect them and yourself. If you have a DSM (Don't Shoot Me) banner, this is the best time to prominently display it to alert responding law enforcement that you are one of the good guys.

The armed defender will start by having their firearm out and pointed at the ready or toward any perceive threat or unknown area where a threat could emanate from. Instruct the person you are shielding to stand or crouch *directly behind you.*

The person you are shielding will grab onto the back of your belt with one hand and place their other hand on your back between your shoulder blades. This positioning will facilitate both of you as you move. The person will be capable of keeping pace step for step with you as you stand; shuffle step moving left, right, or forward; or squat to take cover as you move through the dangerous environment.

The person you are shielding can look sideways and behind you to your blind spots and can alert you to threats simply by calling out the threat and the relative position. As an example, the person could say, "Behind you!" The armed defender can then turn to address the threat.

If there are more than one person in need of protection by armed shielding, the additional person can form a chain by holding onto the person in front of them. The third (or subsequent) persons can grab onto the back of the belt of the person in front of them with one hand and place their other hand on the person's back between their shoulder blades.

Tape Loop:

Many people who have experienced and survived an incident involving the death or near death of themselves, or one or more persons due to an act of violence, will usually later remember the incident in relative detail and usually in the true order the events took place. Due to the sheer terror of the moments in that incident, the body's adrenaline has performed as it should to assist in surviving the attack. Once the incident is over, the person's adrenaline will gradually decrease and bodily functions return to normal.

The mind however may do some very interesting things over the course of the next several hours after the incident that I refer to as a "tape loop." This occurs when the survivor begins to repeatedly play the incident in their mind and sometimes changes the actual sequence of events.

This unintended mental change from the true order of events can cause self-doubt to the point where the survivor may feel they or others did something wrong and can cause them great mental anguish. Knowing in advance that this "tape loop" may replay the events in their mind not as how they actually occurred, but in an alternate sequence of events may help the survivor to know that sometimes the mind may play tricks and create self-doubt. The survivor may need to rely on friends, family, and co-workers who truly know them and may be able to confirm their belief and faith in the survivor that they in fact did the right things during the ordeal.

I would strongly encourage any person who has been involved in an incident as a survivor, or where one or more persons perished or nearly perished to seek professional help. Survivors need to know that whatever they did to live through the incident, they did it right because they survived the attack!

Conclusion

We live in a world that can be both miraculous and dangerous. Most of us are social animals who prefer to be around people and go to public places rather than live as hermits. We frequent public places and areas as we work, play, attend places of worship, school, and special events such as concerts, festivals, sporting events, and countless other social gatherings. We eat in restaurants, go to movie theaters, and occasionally go on vacations to beautiful places to enjoy the benefits of a relaxing environment, many of which may have become gun-free zones.

All these types of places have experienced violent attacks from active shooters in the recent and not too distant past. And if it has not happened there before, it still could occur. Past shooters have either researched the active shooters before them to copycat one or more of their methods or have chosen to strike out on their own and use their own creative thoughts to cook up something that has never been seen or done before. Whenever an active shooting occurs throughout our world, many people contemplate the motives of the killer. The killer may or may not express their true motives for committing their despicable acts of violence. One fact is abundantly clear; the killer had a capacity to commit evil acts unto others that was not apparent to others until that fateful day.

Whenever you are around people and living your best life, don't be so fearful that you are unable to enjoy yourself. However, you must <u>stay vigilant</u> by keeping your eyes and ears open <u>should you notice danger</u>

<u>signs</u> that lead you to believe that things have gone or about to go upside down around you due to an active shooter/assailant. And if you do notice danger signs, take the necessary actions to stay safe.

As we venture out into public, we expect people who are charged with our safety to have taken all (not just some) of the steps necessary to protect us from physical harm. On one end of the spectrum, a few places will have taken the threat seriously or adopted the appropriate steps, sought out and incorporated active shooter defense training, and have many levels and proper safeguards in place.

On that opposite end of the spectrum, there are organizations whose leaders repeatedly fail and refuse to do the right thing for so many reasons, leaving everyone in their environment vulnerable to attack because they purposely neglect to take even the most basic safety precautions.

They either take minimum safety precautions as if they are just checking a box to say they have addressed the issue, or arrogantly refuse to seek out or participate in viable programs that provide valuable information on how they and their people can take assertive steps to protect themselves in the midst of a deadly attack.

Whatever situation you find yourself in, this is your opportunity to educate yourself and the loved ones. You now have the choice and the tools to train yourself and others who are willing to participate in lifesaving techniques and tactics on <u>what to do when, not *if*,</u> this happens in your world. There is no such thing as a fair fight when it comes to defending yourself against a person attempting to take your life or the lives of your family members.

Be prepared to **disarm and disable** any armed person who represents a threat to your life and the lives of your family members.

Nearly all my adult life, I have dedicated and continue to dedicate myself to the protection of others and proven repeatedly that the tactics and techniques I practice actually work! The people who attack, kill, or attempt to kill innocent people are in fact real-life monsters. The numerous cases I provided illustrated examples that these types of killings will probably not stop in the immediate or distant future. After this guide is published, I sadly predict we can expect more of the same from the future active shooters. Past shooting events has taught us that the killing stops only when the killer decides to stop of his or her own accord or when someone (armed or unarmed) competently intervenes to stop the killer.

I leave you with three thoughts:

1. Protect yourself at all times.
2. Do unto bad guys or gals (who intend to do you harm) <u>just before</u> they do unto you.
3. Always and everywhere, be ready!

I have provided a number of checklists that can apply to a variety of business, schools, churches, and many other locations and situations. The checklists provide basic information that could be used as a baseline of security measures all geared toward maximizing safety and options that perhaps you or others may not have considered to defend against an active shooter/assailant.

Acknowledgments

....

I would first like to thank Jesus Christ, my Lord and Savior. Without his hand on my life, God only knows ... I would also like to thank my family and friends, all who have encouraged me and showed their patience through all my trials and tribulations in the quest to provide safety tactics and techniques. I would also like to thank my martial arts instructors, Stanford McNeal, Alexander Archie, Bishop Donnie Williams, and Steve (Sanders) Muhammad. It was through their training and expert tutelage that I acquired my quest for knowledge and obtained technical ability in the martial arts and law enforcement officer safety principles.

I would like to thank everyone who has helped me with this project. Photographers Terri Svetich and Derek Kroshus not only helped with a number of photographs but also numerous training presentations in my undying quest to communicate this information to everyone. I also thank all the models who took time from their busy schedules to help me illustrate the specific tactics or techniques: Boris and Jacob Tavcar, Samantha Joi Walker, Joseph R. Boteler II, Paige Morrell, and Rose Mathews.

I would also like to thank Linda Honey, Nicole Nance, Karyn Jensen, and Paul Reyes, who provided the use of their facilities for several of the photographs. I would like to thank Traci Fox for the use of her critical eye and editing of this work to make it even more of a useful guide.

Active Shooter Defense Checklist

These items can provide suggestions for businesses but can also be used for personal use. Note that many concepts and ideas may overlap.

Organizational Command and Control:

- ➤ Is there a designated organizational chart?
- ➤ Are all managers/supervisors aware of the chain of command via the organizational chart?
- ➤ Do all managers and supervisors have access to contact information and telephone numbers of all top managers per the organizational chart?
- ➤ Who would be designated as the organization's emergency incident commander should a serious critical incident occur?
- ➤ Who is the successor to the emergency Incident Commander?
- ➤ Has the successor to the emergency incident commander been communicated to others within the organization?
- ➤ Has there been training to emergency incident personnel to adequately address natural and man-made incidents such as flood, fires, earthquakes, tornados, active shooters, armed intruders, and so forth?
- ➤ Are top managers and supervisors thoroughly trained in

emergency command processes in the incident command system?

➢ What initiates and establishes the emergency incident commander to be capable of establishing leadership over the incident?

➢ What factors initiate and establishes leadership to relieve the emergency Incident Commander in the event the emergency Incident Commander is incapable, overcome, or the event has been successfully downgraded?

➢ Are there periodic reviews and assessments of the emergency incident commander to ensure competency for all foreseen potential life-altering situations?

➢ Are specific emergency evacuation plans communicated to all employees?

➢ Are specific administrative rally points established for employees who only evacuate for natural disasters (flood, fire, earthquake, and so on)?

➢ Are employees taught to be extra vigilant whenever a fire alarm is activated and to determine if the building evacuation was a ruse for an active shooter?

➢ Are employees advised to follow emergency managers and security personnel or in their absence take the best action for their own survival during an active shooter/assailant assault?

➢ Has significant thought been given as to where to establish a command post during any event that caused the evacuation of the facility?

➢ Are employees advised *not to respond* to a rally point in the event of an active shooter?

➢ Who is authorized to give the all clear signal for your facility?

➢ How is the all clear signaled to all employees?

➢ Is there a silent duress alarm established for a potential problem with "trouble unknown"?

➢ Is there an audible duress code word available for coworkers?

➢ Is there a specific audible alarm for an active shooter/assailant?

- ➢ Is there a free-flowing and situational application of protocol well established and communicated for all employees to follow in the event of an active shooter/assailant?
- ➢ How often are all audible alarms tested and verified?
- ➢ What is the average response time for law enforcement to respond to an emergency in progress?

Exterior of Building:

- ➢ Is the exterior parking area well lighted?
- ➢ Is there video surveillance of the areas?
- ➢ Are trees and shrubs trimmed to prevent suspects from hiding?
- ➢ Is the front door or entry door well marked?
- ➢ Is there an employee only entrance?
- ➢ How is the employee entrance protected to only allow employee access?
- ➢ Is there a no weapons policy for the facility and signage posted?
- ➢ Is visitor parking designated?
- ➢ Are visitors directed where to enter the facility?
- ➢ Are there alarm duress buttons strategically placed throughout the lot?
- ➢ Do security officers patrol the exterior of the facility?
- ➢ Are security personnel trained to spot, respond to, and properly address all unusual physical appearances to the building?
- ➢ Are security personnel armed and capable of addressing an active shooter?

Physical Security and Integrity of the Facility:

- ➢ What types of physical barriers are erected to prevent a vehicle attacking and breaching the facility doors?
- ➢ What type of front door is in place?
- ➢ Is the front door entrance area comprised of wood or glass?
- ➢ Are cameras capable of being viewed on and off site via a

smartphone?

- ➤ Is there a specific audible alarm for an in-progress active shooter event?
- ➤ Is there a silent visual alarm system for a duress alarm?
- ➤ Are there controlled points of entry?
- ➤ Are there signs throughout the facility that advise all of the following: "If you see something, say something and do something"?
- ➤ Are there surveillance cameras located throughout the facility?
- ➤ Are the surveillance cameras strategically located?
- ➤ Is there a designated place for employees and guests to enter?
- ➤ Are you using traditional locks and keys, key cards, or cypher locks?
- ➤ How is key handle controlled?
- ➤ How often are key audits or combinations changed?
- ➤ Are there places for weapons screening at the controlled entry points?
- ➤ Are there provisions for legally armed persons to check their firearms?
- ➤ Are visitors required to sign in and be badged?
- ➤ Does your staff know how to challenge or redirect lost or wandering guests?
- ➤ Do you have designated places for deliveries?
- ➤ Is there a person to escort and observe all deliveries into the facility?
- ➤ Are those delivery door points controlled to ensure entrances only allow controlled access of the deliveries?
- ➤ Is there a receptionist at the front or main entrance?
- ➤ Are the receptionist and relieving personnel trained to deal with hostile individuals and the presence of illegally armed persons?
- ➤ Do your personnel know how to handle a telephonic bomb threat?

> Does the facility have a specific active shooter audible alarm?
> Are there multiple locations where the active shooter alarm can be activated?
> Who else on the staff has access to the active shooter alarms?
> Does everyone on staff know what to do if/when the active shooter alarm is activated?
> Does the staff know how to disarm and disable an armed threat?
> Is the staff knowledgeable about identifying improvised weapons?
> Does your staff have access to a hard room (a place where the walls and doors are somewhat fortified and offer greater protection) where they can shelter in place?
> How and under what circumstances will an all clear be given for the active shooter alarm?

Administrative Area and Controls:

> Is there a physical barrier to restrict unauthorized personnel or unwanted and unscheduled visitors?
> Is there a receptionist for the administrative area?
> Are there methods to establish and designate a guest of the facility?
> Are there policies to ensure all guests are always escorted?
> Is there a duress code word to signal danger to employees?
> Are all employees trained on how to respond/react to a duress alarm?
> Are all employees trained on how to respond/react to an audible active shooter alarm?
> Are all employees trained on how to respond/react to an actual active shooter?
> Is there a policy requiring all employees to register a change of address and telephone number within forty-eight hours?
> Does management have an up-to-date list of all employees with

their current addresses and telephone numbers?

> Can management access employee residential information from off-site?
> Do managers have a bug-out bag for emergencies?
> Are managers trained on bleeding control for trauma injuries?
> Are there bleeding control emergency trauma kits located throughout the facility?
> Do all trained managers have their own bleeding control trauma kits?

Security Personnel:

> Are the property jurisdictional lines clear in the minds of all security personnel?
> Are security personnel uniformed or in plain clothes?
> Are security personnel armed or unarmed?
> Are the firearms carried by security personnel of sufficient caliber to stop an armed intruder?
> How competent are the security personnel with their firearms?
> How often are the security personnel attending range training?
> Do security personnel have access to at least one long gun?
> Are security officers properly equipped with other equipment, including ballistic vests, handcuffs, flashlights, radios with earpieces, additional ammunition, and so forth?
> Are security personnel capable of observing and responding to unusual or suspicious violent activity and do they know when to call for police response and make arrests for violent offenses?
> How often do security personnel attend active shooter defense training?
> Does a representative of management attend the training with security to observe their preparedness?
> How are security personnel summoned to respond to a problem location?

- Does the security office have the capability for temporary storage of licensed concealed firearms?
- Are security personnel trained to notice the signs of a person carrying a concealed firearm?
- Are security personnel trained to mitigate hostile situations?
- Are security personnel required to be present in the immediate area for all employee discipline and discharge issues?
- Are there protocols for employee discipline and discharge?
- Are security personnel trained to spot mentally disturbed individuals?
- Are security personnel trained to spot obvious criminal elements and activity?
- How do security personnel respond to panic or duress alarms?
- Is there a dispatcher on-site to interact with security personnel and to keep a log and facilitate communication between security personnel and police dispatchers?
- Is there a central location for surveillance cameras to be viewed by the on-site dispatcher?
- Are security personnel trained how and when to communicate safety concerns to their on-site dispatcher or to summon police assistance?
- Is there an emergency code that security personnel can use to advise and request expedited response from law enforcement?
- Are security personnel trained how to direct employees during building evacuation, shelter in place, and so forth?
- Is there a liaison between security management and local law enforcement?
- Does the liaison regularly meet with local law enforcement to express concerns and work out potential issues in advance?
- Are security personnel trained in basic first aid?
- Are security personnel trained in bleeding control for traumatic injuries?
- Are security personnel mandated to write reports?

> ➢ Under what criteria are security personnel mandated to complete written reports?
> ➢ Are there supervisors designated to review to approve/reject and direct personnel to rewrite all security reports if necessary? The supervisory approval process is meant to review reports for accuracy.

Individual Offices:

> ➢ Is there a vast amount of glass leading to the interior office areas?
> ➢ Are there window coverings (blinds or window shades) to restrict the view of the office interior and the interior hallway areas?
> ➢ Are the doors for the offices solid core, hollow core, or glass?
> ➢ Is there any type of locking device that can be deployed to barricade the office door (night lock type of device)?
> ➢ If the office is located on the ground level, is there glass leading to the outside?
> ➢ Is there anything the occupant can use to break the glass and use the window for an emergency escape route?
> ➢ If the office is located on a second floor with a window, is there an emergency evacuation ladder available?
> ➢ Is there anything (hammer, heavy paperweight, baseball bat, or so forth) that the occupant can use as an improvised weapon should the shooter breach the barricaded office?
> ➢ Are office occupants educated on how to obtain improvised environmental weapons to use against an active shooter?
> ➢ Are office occupants taught how to properly hide to ambush the shooter should the shooter breach the location?
> ➢ Is the office furniture arranged to provide maximum protection to the occupant in the event of an active shooter, with the office desk positioned outside the fatal funnel?

Hard Rooms (Places of Refuge to Barricade or Sequester):

> - Are there designated hard rooms located in your facility?
> - Is there more than one hard room?
> - Is the room adequately protected from shots being fired into the hard room (does it have armored and protected doors and walls, no glass, and so forth)?
> - Is there a bleeding control emergency trauma kit inside the room?
> - Does the hard room have several power outlets and various cell phone charging cables?
> - Will cell phones function inside the hard room?
> - Is there bottled water and a limited food supply on hand?
> - Does the hard room have a supply of plastic garbage bags for waste disposal?
> - Are there improvised weapons (tool kits, screwdrivers, hammers, wrenches, box cutters, scissors, and so forth) that can be used?
> - Can occupants inside the hard room access surveillance cameras of the facility to view and locate the exact position of the intruder/shooter?
> - Is there a possible escape route from the hard room or is it the only one way in and out?

Lockdown Corridors:

> - Have you calculated the amount of employees locked down in each area?
> - How are employees taught to react to a lockdown status?
> - Are there alternate avenues of escape available from the lockdown area?
> - Do personnel have ample improvised environmental weapons available?

➤ Have there been armed personnel allocated for each lockdown corridor?

➤ Have personnel been taught how to use those weapons to ambush?

➤ Are there additional supplies (food, water, waste disposal) for lengthy periods?

Staff Employees/Personnel:

➤ Is there an employee only entrance?

➤ Is there a designated employee parking area?

➤ Is the designated employee parking area controlled or accessible to anyone?

➤ How are former employees or other members of the general public restricted from entering the employee parking area?

➤ How are former employees restricted from entering the facility?

➤ Is there a person who checks the identification and validity of all persons who represent themselves as employees?

➤ What is the protocol for former employees who approach the employee entrance?

➤ Is there a "do not admit" list complete with names and photographs for either disgruntled former employees or members of the general public?

➤ Are there protocols developed for a "do not admit" person?

➤ Is there a panic button that emits both a visual and audible alarm if activated?

➤ Are employees screened for the presence of firearms as they enter the facility?

➤ How would any employee signal signs of duress to peers and/or security?

➤ Are security personnel stationed at areas where employees enter and exit the facility?

➤ Are there surveillance cameras strategically placed at all locations where employees enter and exit the building?

➤ What methods are used to determine guests of the facility?

➤ Are staff adequately trained on how to direct unaccompanied guests?

➤ Are staff trained on how to shelter in place if evacuation is not possible?

➤ Are staff trained how to protect visitors within their control to either shelter or follow their directions in the event of an emergency or escape?

➤ Does every staff member have access to an LED flashlight?

Business Continuity of Operations Plan (COOP):

➤ Does the business have a current COOP?

➤ Who is in charge of updating the COOP?

➤ What are the lines of succession and are they clearly spelled out to top management officials?

➤ Does all leadership know where the primary and secondary relocation sites are?

➤ Do all personnel who are required to relocate to the alternate site know when and where to relocate?

➤ When was the last time personnel exercised relocating to a different site?

➤ Do personnel exercise plans with realistic issues and scenarios such as the presence of an active shooter, workplace violence, fire, earthquake, and so on?

➤ How often is the COOP exercised?

➤ Is there a complete and updated roster of all employees, complete with addresses and telephone numbers?

➤ Do employee records show a next of kin for each employee?

➤ Are all top management officials capable of retrieving employee rosters when they are off-site?

➤ How are missing personnel accounted for?

Facility Restrooms:

> - Are public restrooms locked?
> - Is the locking device a key or cypher lock?
> - How often is the cypher lock combination changed?
> - Is the restroom door a solid core door?
> - Is there a deadbolt installed for all restroom doors for interior locking?
> - Is there a peephole installed to look from the inside to the outside area?
> - Are the restrooms periodically swept to ensure no dangerous materials are left behind (suspicious packages)?
> - Are there potential items inside the restrooms that could be used as improvised weapons?
> - Will cell phones function inside the restrooms?

Special Events:

> - Are there adequate security personnel available to manage the entrance of the event?
> - Is there a sufficient quantity of security personnel available to handle the security inside the event?
> - Are all security personnel properly equipped with ballistic vest, handcuffs, flashlights, radios with earpieces, firearms, additional ammunition, and so forth)?
> - Are security personnel in easily identifiable uniforms?
> - Is there an event dispatcher to be used for all radio communications for security personnel?
> - Are your security personnel armed?
> - Are security personnel at all entrances and exits?
> - Are all exits covered to ensure that illegal/unauthorized entry is restricted?
> - Are there operational metal detection devices available at all entrances?

- ➤ Are personnel qualified to operate metal detection devices?
- ➤ Are all personnel entering the facility screened to ensure no weapons are or have been smuggled inside?
- ➤ Have explosive detection dogs been deployed at entrances?
- ➤ Have explosive detection dogs conducted a sweep of the area prior to attendance of guests?
- ➤ Is there a protocol established for a security breach?
- ➤ Are there provisions for entry of legally armed law enforcement personnel (active duty and retired)?
- ➤ Are security personnel conducting face-to-face meetings with all non-uniformed personnel allowed to be armed within the facility during the event?
- ➤ How are legally armed law enforcement personnel (off duty and retired) equipped to be identified during a critical incident?
- ➤ Who is in charge of security during the event?
- ➤ If the event becomes too unruly, what is the protocol for cancelling the event or requesting assistance from police?
- ➤ Are there sufficient exits for all persons entering the venue?

Threat Assessment Team:

- ➤ Is the team comprised of knowledgeable and competent individuals dedicated to the safety of those in their charge?
- ➤ Is there a protocol established for the team to operate?
- ➤ Does management recognize the value and recommendations of the team?
- ➤ How often does the team meet to discuss issues?
- ➤ What types of situations come before the threat assessment team?
- ➤ How streamlined are the team's recommendations?
- ➤ How quickly can the team meet to discuss an emergency?
- ➤ Is a written report mandatory?
- ➤ How long does it take to render a decision and to communicate to leadership?

Armed Non–Law Enforcement Defender on Premises (this is a person or persons employed by a company, *not* a law enforcement agency):

> ➤ Is the armed defender reputable?
> ➤ Is the armed defender physically and mentally fit?
> ➤ What is the temperament of the armed defender?
> ➤ Does the background of the armed defender reflect a significant law enforcement career?
> ➤ Is the armed defender competent with their firearm?
> ➤ Is it required that the armed defender has a LEOSA qualification from a local law enforcement agency stipulating that he or she has a current concealed weapons LEOSA carry permit?
> ➤ Is it known exactly how many personnel are allowed to be armed on the premises?
> ➤ Are the armed defenders proportioned throughout the facility?
> ➤ How much training has been provided to the armed defender on active shooter defense?
> ➤ Is the armed defender's weapon of sufficient caliber to stop an active shooter?
> ➤ Does the armed defender carry additional equipment such as a flashlight, radio, extra ammunition, ballistic vest, cellular telephone, Bluetooth (hands-free device), a second weapon, and so forth?
> ➤ Is the weapon carried by the armed defender concealed?
> ➤ How are the permitted armed defenders introduced to other employees?
> ➤ Does the armed defender have access to secondary weapons and a long gun if necessary?
> ➤ How often are the armed defenders attending range training?
> ➤ How competent are the armed defenders with their firearms?
> ➤ Do the armed defenders know the rules of engagement against an active shooter/assailant?

> ➢ Has a liaison been established between the organization/ business and the local law enforcement agencies?
> ➢ Have safety protocols been set up for the armed defender to protect them from the friendly fire of responding officers?
> ➢ Will the armed defender be in civilian clothing, a uniform, or have any identifying markers to depict they are friendly?
> ➢ Is the armed defender known to all employees?
> ➢ How are armed defenders able to help responding law enforcement distinguish between friend and foe?

Post–Shooting Event: (To be used by either by a person or an organizational administrative designee)

> ➢ Is the environment deemed safe?
> ➢ Who are the injured persons?
> ➢ Is the shooter down or appear to have fled the scene?
> ➢ If the shooter is down, is the shooter incapacitated?
> ➢ If the shooter is down and not incapacitated, is the shooter disarmed?
> ➢ Have emergency trauma services been summoned?
> ➢ Is law enforcement on scene?
> ➢ Are there restricted areas that you need to access to obtain personal belongings?
> ➢ Have you checked with law enforcement prior to moving throughout the scene before retrieving personal property?
> ➢ Will you be able to leave the crime scene safely?
> ➢ Have you fully examined yourself to determine that you have no physical injuries?
> ➢ If you require medical attention, have you communicated with the hospital where you intend to be treated?
> ➢ Are there others within the environment for whom you need to ensure their mental and physical safety?
> ➢ From a work perspective, do you have contact numbers of

individuals that need to be contacted?

- ➤ Do you have a contact for your local Red Cross office for possible deployment for your employees or family?
- ➤ Do you have next of kin information accessible for your affected employees?
- ➤ Is your next of kin contact information up to date?
- ➤ Can you access computer files where you can work from home or another alternate site?
- ➤ Do you have access to your personal items such as keys, wallet, and cell phone?
- ➤ Will you require transportation from the scene or anywhere else on your route home?
- ➤ Have you advised your spouse or significant other as to what has occurred?
- ➤ Do you need to speak to other family members aside from your spouse or significant other?
- ➤ Can you telephone friends or family to arrange for transportation?
- ➤ Have you advised friends or family members of your current condition/circumstances?
- ➤ Can you obtain clean clothing if your clothing has been soiled or taken by law enforcement for evidence?
- ➤ Will you need to obtain clothing or personal hygiene items?
- ➤ Do you have access to funds for foods and medicine to sustain you for several days if necessary?
- ➤ Do you have a primary care physician to consult?
- ➤ Do you need to speak with anyone in the immediate future regarding your current mental condition?
- ➤ Do you have a personal psychologist or other mental health professional?
- ➤ Have you begun the process of critical incident debriefing for persons involved?
- ➤ Do you have close friends or relatives with whom you might

spend the next several hours?

➤ Keep in mind that the "tape loop" may replay several hours later and to not allow the altered sequence of events of the tape loop to influence your future actions.

Post-Shooting items to avoid:

➤ Resist the urge to relive the event by watching it on television, listening to the news over the radio, or viewing it on social media.

➤ Do not submit to an interview by any media person or outlet.

➤ Do not write or respond to anything on social media about the event.

➤ You may be advised of your rights per Miranda warning. If so, are you prepared to provide to a law enforcement agency a brief oral or written account of what occurred?

➤ If you have taken any action that directly or indirectly resulted in a loss of life or serious injury, do you know any criminal defense attorneys who may need to consult with you prior to or during any potential law enforcement interviews?

➤ Do not provide anything in any written format to anyone other than the law enforcement agency investigating the case.

➤ If you took any action that participated in any type of force, remember that the investigation will take a significant amount of time. With that said, be advised of your right to remain silent.

➤ You may never know what and how statements you make may be against your best interest.

About the Author

As the owner of Leading Edge Threat Mitigation and disarmanddisable. com, Joseph B. Walker (preferring to be called Joey) provides real-world tactical and technical information on how to mitigate any number of threats from an active shooter, protection against stalkers, and self-defense courses for civilian and law enforcement personnel. Joey utilizes his expertise as a tenth-degree black belt in the martial arts with two world karate champions to formulate techniques that are practical, easy, and effective against violent assailants. Joey is also the author of two other books: *Self-Defense Tactics and Techniques* and *Shots Fired: Surviving an Active Shooter/Assailant.* The latter was created to help organizations and the average individual attacked by a terrorist or a mentally challenged offender bent on death and destruction. Joey has trained numerous federal, state, local agencies, and private businesses on many of the tactics and techniques to mitigate or defeat the active shooter. He continues to appear on numerous local radio and television stations, covering threat mitigation strategies from stalking, workplace violence, and defense against an active shooter/assailant.

During his twenty-five-year law enforcement career with the Reno Police Department, Joey worked with the Los Angeles Police Department's Gang Unit the Threat Management Unit and authored the "Police Officer's Guide to Stalking" handbook for the Reno Police Department. Joey was a member of the Reno Police Honor Guard, where he performed on numerous occasions as a semi-professional trumpet player at the National Law Enforcement Peace Officers Memorial in Washington, DC, and the Nevada State Peace Officers Memorial. Joey was certified as a physical fitness instructor by the FBI and provided martial arts instruction to the Washoe County Sheriff's Department and Reno Police Department Defensive Tactics Instructors as well as a host of local, state, and federal law enforcement agencies. He has performed dignitary protection and threat assessments for President Gerald Ford, Bernice King, Martin Luther King III, Merle-Evers Williams, and Hank Aaron.

Upon retiring from the Reno Police Department, Joey worked for the United States Department of Homeland Security, where he provided training for several state and federal agencies on active shooter defense and the threat of shoulder-fired missiles.

Joey attended training on Behavior Detection and Small Unit Tactics Training and Dignitary Protection. Due to his extensive background in the martial arts, threat mitigation, law enforcement defensive tactics, and use of force options, Mr. Walker is sought out for criminal and civil trials as well as case preparations as an expert witness within these fields of expertise.